THE STANDARD ENCYCLOPEDIA OF

Opalescent Glass

IDENTIFICATION & VALUES

BILL EDWARDS

COLLECTOR BOOKS

A Division of Schroeder Publishing Co., Inc.

Searching for a Publisher?

We are always looking for knowledgeable people considered to be experts within their fields. If you feel that there is a real need for a book on your collectible subject and have a large comprehensive collection, contact Collector Books.

On the Cover:

Fluted Scrolls Spooner, vaseline opalescent (Northwood)
Compass Plate, blue opalescent (Dugan/Diamond)
Wide Panel Epergne, green opalescent (Northwood)

Cover design by Beth Summers
Book design by Terri Stalions

Additional copies of this book may be ordered from:

Collector Books
P.O. Box 3009
Paducah, Kentucky 42002-3009

@$19.95. Add $2.00 for postage and handling.
Copyright: Bill Edwards, 1995

Inquiries (with SASE) may be sent to:
Bill Edwards
620 W. 2nd St.
Madison, IN 47250

Dedication

In memory of Byron Rinehart who, along with his wife, Grace, has given a lifetime to glass collecting. And to Lucile and John Britt whose years of friendship are treasured. They've always shared their knowledge and glass whenever I've asked.

Acknowledgments

A book such as this one depends on the generosity of many people and this book is no exception. I gratefully acknowledge the help of the following: Preston VerMeer and Jack Beckwith who allowed me access to their collections and to Dennis Addy who photographed the Beckwith glass. And to Mike Carwile, Bill Banks, John and Lucile Britt, Pat and Bob Davis, the Lumber Mill Antique Mall, the Broadway Antique Mall, Mary Breeck, Bonnie and Richard Boldt, as well as anyone I may have unintentionally overlooked.

Author's Note

When I wrote the *Standard Opalescent Price Guide* in 1992, I wasn't prepared for the dozens and dozens of letters from collectors who wanted an expanded book on opalescent glass, so it is with a great deal of pride that I present this companion book to my *Standard Encyclopedia of Carnival Glass.* I consider it the best of all my many books over the years and I hope collectors will agree. I could not have accomplished such a task in the two years of research and writing if I hadn't had the aid of many opalescent collectors, the encouragement of my publisher and editor, and the photos that are mentioned in the acknowledgment section.

This is my twenty-first publication, 20 of which have been produced by Collector Books and I am happy to have had such a fine working relationship with very good people. When I wrote that first Millersburg book in 1974, I had no idea such a lengthy relationship could or would come about and I am forever grateful for the friendship and patience of the Schroeders. I hope I'm still working on a book for them when the Lord calls me home.

Bill Edwards

Contents

Part I: Opalescent
Glass, 1880 – 1930
Page 8

Part II: Opalescent
Whimsies
Page 96

Part III: Opalescent
Glass After 1930
and Reproductions
Page 106

Introduction

From its inception in the 1880s opalescent glass has enjoyed a widely receptive audience, both in England where it was introduced and here in America where a young but growing market was ready for any touch of brightness and beauty for the hearth and home.

Early American makers, such as Hobbs, Brockunier and Company (1863 – 1888), Buckeye Glass (1878 – 1896), LaBelle Glass (1872 – 1888), American Glass (1889 – 1891), Nickel Plate Glass (1888 – 1893), and of course, the Northwood Glass Company in its various locations (1888 until its demise in 1924) were the primary producers, especially in early blown opalescent glass production. They were not by themselves, of course. Other companies such as Model Flint (1893 – 1899), Fostoria Shade & Lamp Co. (1890 – 1894), Consolidated Lamp & Glass (1894 – 1897), Elson Glass (1882 – 1893), West Virginia Glass (1893 – 1896), National Glass (1899 – 1903), Beaumont Glass (1895 – 1906), Dugan Glass (1904 – 1913) which then became Diamond Glass (1914 – 1931); and finally the Jefferson Glass Company (1900 – 1933) added their talents in all sorts of opalescent items in both blown and pressed glass.

The major production covered 40 years (1880 – 1920); however beginning shortly after the turn of the century the Fenton Glass Company of Williamstown, West Virginia, joined the ranks of opalescent manufacturers and has continued production off and on until the present time. Their production from 1907 to 1940 is an important part of the opalescent field and has been covered to some extent in this book. The Fenton factory, along with Dugan and Jefferson glass, produced quality opalescent glass items long after the rest of the companies had ceased operations, primarily in pressed items in patterns they had used for other types of glassware.

To understand just what opalescent glass is has always been easy; to explain the process of making this glass is quite another matter. If the novice will think of two layers of glass, one colored and one clear, that have been fused so that the clear areas become milky when fired a second or third time, the picture of the process becomes easier to see. It is, of course, much more complicated than that but for the sake of clarity, imagine the clear layer being pressed so that the second firing gives this opal milkyness to the outer edges, be they design or the edges themselves, and the process becomes clearer. It is, of course, the skill of the glassmaker to control this opalescence so that it does what he wants. It is a fascinating process and anyone who has had the privilege of watching a glassmaker at work can testify to it being a near-miracle.

Today, thousands of collectors seek opalescent glass and each has his or her own favorites. Current markets place blown opalescent glass as more desirable, with cranberry leading the color field, but there are many ways to collect, and groupings of one shape or one pattern or even one manufacturer are not uncommon. When you purchase this glass the same rules apply as any other glass collectible: (1) look for any damage and do not pay normal prices for damage; (2) choose good color as well as good milky opalescence; (3) **Buy what pleases you!** You have to live with it, so buy what you like. To care for your glass, wash it carefully in lukewarm water and a mild soap; **Never put old glass in a dishwasher!** Display your glass in an area that is well lighted and enjoy it!

Who Made It?

Confusion abounds over the Northwood/National/Dugan connection, as well as the Jefferson/Northwood connection. In 1896 Harry Northwood, Samuel Dugan Sr., and his sons Thomas, Alfred, and Samuel Dugan Jr. came to Indiana, Pennsylvania, operating the Northwood Glass Company there until 1899, when Harry Northwood joined the newly-formed National Glass company combine. In 1903, he moved his operation to Wheeling at the old Hobbs, Brockunier plant and Thomas Dugan remained at the Indiana plant operating it as the Dugan Glass company.

From 1896 on, several patterns were produced as first Northwood, then National, and finally as Dugan; patterns such as Argonaut Shell/Nautilus, for example. There were many others that have previously been classified as either Northwood or Dugan that are actually Northwood/National/Dugan or even National/Dugan.

In addition we have certain patterns duplicated by both Jefferson and Northwood with little explanation as to why moulds that were once Jefferson's then became Northwood's. Both companies were competitors, but examples of some patterns can be traced to both companies. It is also evident most patterns with a cranberry edging are really Jefferson, not Northwood as once believed.

Every answer raises new questions and in my 25 years of researching and writing about glass, I've learned that patience is the key. Answers come in their own time and at their own pace. One day we'll know most of what we question today and that is what drives us. I learn every day, mostly by contact with other collectors and so, I'm sure, do all of you.

Part I:
Opalescent Glass, 1880 – 1930

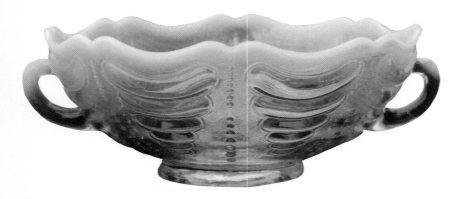

Abalone

Acorn Burrs

Abalone
Found only in bowls with small solid handles, the Abalone pattern is believed to be from the Jefferson Glass Company and dates from the 1902 – 1905 period. Colors are blue, white, green, and rarely canary opalescent glass. The design, a series of graduated arcs in column, separated by a line of bubble-like dots, is nice, but nothing special.

Acorn Burrs
Here is another of those well-known Northwood patterns that was made in the 1907 – 09 era in very limited opalescent glass production. Acorn Burrs is found in carnival glass in many shapes such as table sets, water sets, and berry sets. In opalescent glass it is limited to the small berry bowl shape and possibly the larger bowl (though none have been confirmed to date). Opalescent colors seem be just as limited and these small bowls are known in white and blue.

Alaska

Alaska

One of the early Northwood patterns, Alaska dates from 1897, and can be found in a wide range of shapes including table sets, water sets, berry sets, a cruet, banana boat, celery tray, shakers, bride's basket. The tumblers and shakers are interchangeable with plain Fluted Scrolls and Jackson pieces. Colors are blue, white, vaseline, and emerald green as well as plain and decorated crystal.

Arabian Nights

Dating from 1895 or 1896, this Northwood pattern, while confined to water sets and a syrup, can be found in white, blue, canary, and cranberry opalescent glass. The design (swirls, blossoms, and dots) combines the best of both Spanish Lace and Daisy and Fern and is a very striking pattern.

Argonaut Shell (Nautilus)

Originally a Northwood pattern, the opalescent examples were made by National or by Dugan after Northwood left National. Colors are blue, white, and vaseline and the shapes include water sets, table sets, berry sets, compotes, shakers, novelty bowls, and a cruet.

Arabian Nights

Argonaut Shell

Astro

Aurora Borealis

A stro

Primarily a bowl pattern, Astro was made by the Jefferson Glass Company about 1905. It is a simple design of six circular comet-like rings on a threaded background above three rings of beads that are grouped from the lower center of the bowl upward. Colors are blue, green, white, and canary.

A urora Borealis

Made by the Jefferson Glass Company and dating from 1903, this vase pattern is very typical of stemmed vases in the opalescent glass era. Rising from a notched base the stem widens with a series of bubble and scored lines that end in a flame-shaped top. From the sides are three handle-like projections, giving the whole conception a very nautical feeling. Colors are white, green, and blue opalescent.

A utumn Leaves

I am very drawn to this beautiful bowl pattern, attributed to the Northwood Company from 1905. The colors reported are white and blue opalescent and the design is quite good with large, well-veined leaves around the bowl, connected by twisting branches and a single leaf in the bowl's center.

Autumn Leaves

Baby Coinspot

*B*aby Coinspot

While the well-known syrup in Baby Coinspot is from the Belmont Glass Company and dates from 1887, a newer copy is known by Fenton. The 7" vase shown does not appear to be a new item. The glass is thin and light and the color very soft. It may be that this vase is not American at all but a product of English origin, but I'm sure someone will write me about it. At any rate, it is a very attractive vase and certainly caught my eye.

*B*arbells

Known only in the bowl shape, this rather undistinguished pattern has been credited to the Jefferson Glass Company in the 1905 – 06 period. The main design is a series of vertical ribs topped by a bullseye, with a smaller series of bullseyes below the ribs. Colors are blue, green, white, and canary.

*B*eaded Cable

This well-known Northwood pattern can be found in several treatments including opalescent, carnival, and custard. In opalescent glass, the colors are blue, green, white, and canary. Both rose bowls and open bowls are from the same mould. The design is simple yet effective and dates from 1904.

Barbells

Beaded Cable

Beaded Drapes

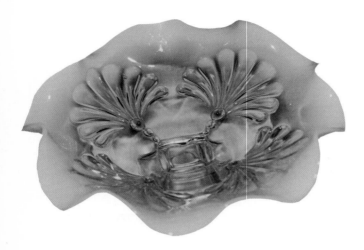

Beaded Fans

Beaded Fleur de Lis

Beaded Drapes

This very attractive pattern is thought to be from the Northwood Company although examples with cranberry edging like some Jefferson items can be found. Dating from 1905, the pattern can be found on footed bowls, rose bowls, and banana bowls in blue, green, white, and vaseline.

Beaded Fans

Found mostly on footed rose bowls from the same mould as the bowl shown, this pattern is exactly like Shell and Dots minus the dotted base. Colors are white, green, and blue and the pattern dates from 1905. It has been credited to Northwood, but it is shown in Jefferson Glass ads as #211, so we know it is a Jefferson pattern.

Beaded Fleur de Lis

Attributed to Jefferson Glass, this stemmed compote can be found with the top opened out or turned in like a rose bowl. It was made in the 1906 era in blue, green, and white. The design is quite good and the base is very distinctive with three wide feet and beaded rings on the stems.

Beaded Stars

Beaded Stars

The opalescent version of this pattern was made by the Fenton Glass Company in 1907. Shapes reported are bowls, rose bowls, and a rare plate. Both the bowl and the plate are known in advertising items (the plate is shown elsewhere) and are very rare. Colors found are white, blue, and green in opalescent glass, crystal, and carnival colors.

Beads and Bark

Shown as early as 1903, this Northwood pattern was made in their "Mosaic" or purple slag treatment, as well as appearing in opalescent colors of white, blue, and canary, as well as limited amounts of green. Like so many vases of the time the theme was a rustic look with tree limbs forming the supports to the base. In the case of Beads and Bark, these supports generate into a bowl that is a series of inverted loops with beaded edging forming three rows of design.

Beads and Bark

Beatty Honeycomb

Made by Beatty & Sons in Tiffin, Ohio, the Honeycomb pattern dates to 1888, and is also known as Beatty Waffle. Shapes found are a table set, water set, berry set, cruet, toothpick holder, celery vase, salt shakers, a mustard pot, individual cream and sugar, and the mug shape shown. Colors are white and blue opalescent. Be aware the pattern has been reproduced in the 1960s by the Fenton Glass Company in blue and an emerald green in vases, baskets, rose bowls, and a covered sugar.

Beatty Honeycomb

Beatty Rib

Beatty Swirl

Berry Patch

*B*eatty Rib

The A.J. Beatty & Sons Company originally made glass in Steubenville, Ohio, until they merged with U.S. Glass and moved their operation to Tiffin, Ohio, in 1891. Beatty Rib dates from 1889, and was made in both blue and white in a vast array of shapes including table sets, water sets, berry sets in two shapes, a celery vase, mug, nappies in assorted shapes, salt and pepper shakers, a mustard jar, salt dips, sugar shaker, toothpick holder, finger bowl, match holder, cracker jar, and the rare cigar ashtray.

*B*eatty Swirl

Like its sister pattern, Beatty Rib, this popular design was produced in 1889, in blue, white, and occasionally canary opalescent glass. Shapes known are table sets, water sets, berry sets, syrup, mug, water tray, and celery vase. Other pieces might well have been made including shakers, toothpick holder, cruet, mustard pot, and sugar shaker, so be aware of this possibility.

*B*erry Patch

Here is another of Jefferson's opalescent novelties that is delicate and quite simple in concept but very attractive. Mostly seen in small shallow bowls with a dome base, the design has occasionally been flattened into a dome-based plate that is most desirable. Colors are white, blue, and green opalescent and the pattern was originally Jefferson's #261, dating from 1905. The design is a simple series of stems, leaves, and berry clusters that ramble around the bowl.

*B*lackberry

While the pattern is sometimes called Northwood's Blackberry, I have no doubt it was a pattern produced by the Fenton Glass Company. It has been seen mostly in small sauce shapes but occasionally one of these is pulled into a whimsey shape. Colors in opalescent glass are blue, white, green, and a very pretty amethyst (another indication it is Fenton). It can be found in custard and opaque glass, and many times with a goofus treatment.

*B*locked Thumbprint and Beads

While the history of this pattern tends to be confusing, mainly because it is only one step in a series of patterns done by the Dugan/Diamond Glass Company over a period of time, the study of two closely designed patterns sets the picture in order. Blocked Thumbprint and Beads and another pattern, Leaf Rosette and Beads, are very much alike. When you add a Dugan carnival glass item called Fishscale and Beads to the picture, you can see just why all three patterns came from the same maker. The latter is simply the original Blocked Thumbprint and Beads with an interior pattern of scaling! Opalescent colors are the typical white, blue, and green, but vaseline is a possibility.

*B*looms and Blossoms

Also known as Mikado, this Northwood Glass pattern is known in several treatments including frosted glass with enameling, ruby stained with gilt, the flowers painted in an airy transparent coloring, as well as a goofus treatment. In opalescent glass the usual shape is this square-shaped nappy with one handle. It has been called an olive nappy and can be found in white, green, and blue opalescent colors. And if two names aren't enough, it can also be found as Flower and Bud in some books!

Blackberry

Blocked Thumbprint and Beads

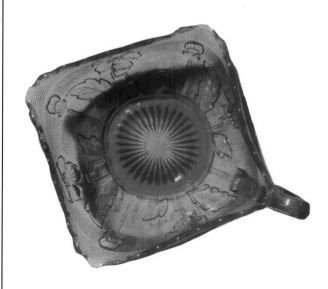

Blooms and Blossoms

15

Blossoms and Palms

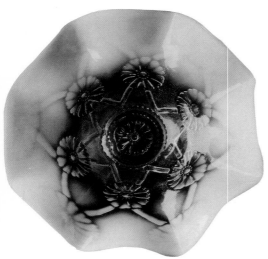

Blossoms and Web

Blown Drapery

Blossoms and Palms

Credited to the Northwood Company, Blossoms and Palms dates to about 1905 and has been reported with the famous Northwood trademark. Colors are blue, white, vaseline, and green, and only bowl shapes have been reported. The design consists of three acanthus-like leaves with a stem of flowers and leaves between them.

Blossoms and Web

This attractive bowl pattern is credited to the Northwood Company and dated to 1905, but I have a hunch it may be a Dugan product. It is found primarily in white opalescent glass, often with a goofus treatment but has been found in blue on rare occasions. The floral design, while very much like Northwood's carnival design of Nippon, also resembles Dugan's Double Stem Rose, as does the method of connecting the flower arrangement.

Blown Drapery

Made by Northwood as part of the National Glass combine in 1903, this very beautiful tankard water set and a companion sugar shaker are mould blown and can be found in white, blue, green, canary, and cranberry opalescent colors. Please compare this set with the later Fenton Drapery set shown elsewhere, for a complete understanding of just how this pattern varies from blown to pressed ware. Also, be aware that Blown Drapery has been reproduced in a cruet shape by L.G. Wright.

Blown Twist

B lown Twist

Made by Northwood, operating as National Glass, this very scarce pattern is known in water sets and a sugar shaker. It dates from 1903 and the colors known are white, blue, canary, green, and cranberry. The handle on the water pitcher has a very unusual twisted look not found on other items in opalescent glass. Please note that the pitcher's mould is the same as that of Blown Drapery (both are blown items).

B oggy Bayou (Reverse Drapery)

Despite all the name confusion over this pattern, we can say with confidence it was originally a bowl pattern that can also be found on plates. The vase was made by the Fenton Art Glass Company in 1907. To add to the confusion, the carnival version of this pattern is called Cut Arcs. Opalescent vases, bowls, and plates can be found in white, blue, green, and amethyst.

B rideshead

This very well done English pattern was made by George Davison Company and bears the Rd #130643 identifying the pattern. Brideshead was made in water sets, table sets, a celery vase, and several bowl novelties in blue with the possibility of both white and canary existing. The pattern is one of alternating concave and convex columns that while simple is quite effective. As you can see, the opalescence is outstanding as is most from English makers.

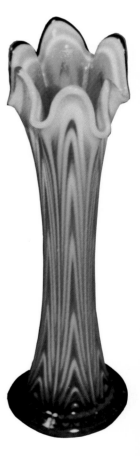

Boggy Bayou

Brideshead

Broken Pillar

Bubble Lattice

Buttons and Braids

Broken Pillar (and Reed)

Broken Pillar and Reed is credited to the Model Flint Glass Company of Albany, Indiana. The pattern dates from the 1902 – 1904 era and originally was called #909. In crystal, amethyst-flashed crystal, and a pretty amber-stained crystal, Broken Pillar and Reed was made in a complete table service as well as a jelly compote, however in opalescent glass, it has been reported only in the compote shape or, as shown, a stemmed card tray fashioned from the compote. Colors reported are white, vaseline, and blue in opalescent glass.

Bubble Lattice

This pattern was called Plaid by Marion Hartung but is more commonly known as Bubble Lattice or simply Lattice. It was made in Wheeling by the Hobbs, Brockunier Company in 1889, and can be found in many shapes including water sets, berry sets, table sets, cruets, sugar shakers, syrups, toothpick holders, finger bowls, salt shakers, bowls, and bride's baskets. Colors are blue, white, canary, and cranberry and the finish was occasionally satinized.

Buttons and Braids

Credited to the Jefferson Company, Buttons and Braids dates to 1905 and has been reported in water sets and bowls in blue, green, white, and cranberry opalescent. Tumblers can be either blown or pressed. In addition to the colors listed, there is a strange greenish vaseline that is very much like some of the Everglades pieces credited to Northwood, so this pattern may well have passed from the Jefferson Company to Northwood like others are known to have done.

Button Panels

Button Panels

Here's a pattern first attributed to the Coudersport Tile & Ornamental Glass Company but shown in Northwood/ National ads in 1902 – 03 and later shown in Dugan/Diamond ads in 1907 – 09. It has often been confused with a similar design called Alaska, but is found only in dome-based bowls and rose bowls. Colors are white, blue, canary, and very rarely green, with emerald known also.

Cabbage Leaf

Exactly like the Winter Cabbage bowl shown elsewhere, except Cabbage Leaf has three large leaf patterns over the twig-like feet. This piece is usually turned up to form a very neat vase. Both patterns are from the Northwood Company and date from its 1906 – 07 period of production. Colors in the Cabbage Leaf pattern are white, green, and blue opalescent with canary a possibility.

Cashews

More commonly found in goofus treatment than opalescent glass, this bowl pattern has been attributed to the Northwood Company. However, I have a hunch it was really made by Dugan after 1904, at the Indiana, PA, factory. Colors are white, blue, and green and the white can be found with some goofus treatment.

Cabbage Leaf

Cashews

Cherry Panels

Chippendale

Christmas Pearls

Cherry Panels (Dugan Cherry)

I apologize for the photo, but felt a picture of the pattern in peach opalescent carnival glass was better than no photo at all. The carnival glass pieces are best known. Besides the footed bowl, there is a collar based bowl (often with Jeweled Heart as an exterior pattern) and plate. In regular opalescent glass the colors are white, blue, and canary with green very possible. These pieces date to 1907, and were among the limited run of opalescent glass the Dugan Company had on patterns that were strong sellers in iridized glass a few years later.

Chippendale

This very pretty pattern was a product of George Davison and Company, England, and dates to 1887. Shapes known are baskets, compotes, and tumblers, so I suspect a jug or pitcher of some shape was made. Colors are blue and canary and both are top notch as the photo clearly shows.

Christmas Pearls

Occasionally called Beaded Panel (it isn't the same as the Beaded Panels pattern often called Opal Open), this quite rare and beautiful pattern is most likely a Jefferson Glass design that dates from 1901 – 1903. The only shapes reported are the cruet shown and a salt shaker. The colors known so far are blue, white, and green opalescent.

Christmas Snowflake

Originally a Hobbs, Brockunier pattern, Christmas Snowflake was a lamp pattern produced by that company in 1891. In 1888, Northwood began production in water sets (both plain and ribbed), as well as, a cruet and possibly a vase. In 1980 a reproduction was made by L.G. Wright of the plain water set, as well as new shapes (sugar shaker, barber bottle, basket, rose bowls in two sizes, syrup, milk pitcher, cruet, brides bowl, and a creamer). The original lamps were made in three sizes in blue, white, and cranberry. The Northwood water set was made in the same colors and the cruet in white only.

Chrysanthemum (Base) Swirl

First made at the Buckeye Glass Company of Martins Ferry, Ohio, this design became one produced by the Northwood Company in a speckled finish. Buckeye production dates to 1890 in white, blue, and cranberry, sometimes with a satin finish. Shapes are water sets, table sets, berry sets, a cruet, syrup, sugar shaker, toothpick holder, salt shaker, finger bowl, celery vase, mustard, and a beautiful straw holder with lid. The speckled treatment was patented by Northwood and except for this look, the shapes are the same.

Chrysanthemum Swirl Variant

Here is a very scarce variant pattern, credited to the Northwood Company by some. It has even been called a mystery variant. In size and make-up, the tankard pitcher is much like Ribbed Opal Lattice, also credited to Northwood from 1888; however if you examine the color of the pitcher here you will find it anything but typical of that company. It isn't blue or even green, but a very strong teal. It can also be found in white and cranberry. It is possible the design was first made elsewhere and Northwood produced later versions.

Christmas Snowflake

Chrysanthemum (Base) Swirl

Chrysanthemum Swirl Variant

Circled Scroll

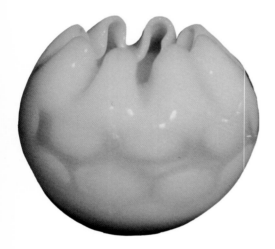

Coinspot (Jefferson)

Coinspot (Northwood)

Circled Scroll

A Dugan Glass product, Circled Scroll dates from 1904 and can be found in carnival glass, opalescent glass, and a soft green glass. Shapes known are the water set, berry set, table set, cruet set, jelly compote, and salt shaker but not all colors are found in each treatment. In the carnival items, a whimsey vase, pulled from a tumbler is also known but none have been reported in opalescent or apple green treatments.

Coinspot (Jefferson)

I believe this previously unreported rose bowl was made by Jefferson from their salad bowl (Jefferson's #83). This company also made the water set (#180) in white, blue, green, and cranberry which was later copied by the Fenton Company. Please note the base which has been ground first.

Coinspot (Northwood)

Shown is the Northwood water pitcher with the star-crimp top. These water sets were made at the Indiana, PA, plant and production was probably continued when Dugan took over the plant. Butler Brothers catalog ads show this pitcher in 1903 – 1904 from the Northwood/National production. Colors are white, blue, green, and cranberry.

Coinspot Syrup

While it is, at best, difficult to distinguish some moulds of one company from those of another, I truly believe the syrup shown is from the West Virginia Glass Company and the same shape can be found in their Polka Dot items where the dots are colored rather than opalescent. At any rate, I'm sure these pieces were made in white, blue, cranberry, and possibly other colors since some Coinspot items are also found in green, amber, vaseline, amberina, rubina, and even amethyst.

Coinspot Water Bottle

In addition to all the other Coinspot items we've shown, I just couldn't resist showing this very scarce water bottle shape. The glass is very light weight and delicate and it has been seen in cranberry opalescent glass, as well as, this white example. While I haven't been able to confirm the maker of this item, I'm confident it is old and quite scarce.

Compass

While this pattern has been identified as Reflecting Diamonds in one publication, it definitely is not. Compass, while similar, has eight large overlapping arcs that make up the key elements of the design while Reflecting Diamonds is a series of graduated petal shapes that contain inverted rays, files, or diamonds topped by more fan rays. Only the marie or base design of the two patterns is the same. Compass is found (very rarely) on large plates in green or blue opalescent and as the exterior of carnival glass bowls with Heavy Grape as the primary design. The plate shown is marked with the Diamond-D mark.

Coinspot Syrup

Coinspot Water Bottle

Compass

Concave Columns

Constellation

Coral

Concave Columns (#617)

As stated elsewhere (see Pressed Coinspot), this pattern was originally called #617 in a 1901 National Glass catalog and was later continued by Dugan/Diamond Glass in an ad assortment in the compote shape. For some strange reason, the vase has become known as Concave Columns. The compote, in opalescent glass is known as Pressed Coinspot and in carnival glass is simply called Coinspot. Shapes from the same mould are vases, compotes, goblets, and a stemmed banana boat shape. Colors in opalescent glass are white, blue, green, and canary. I show both the vase and compote here to clarify just how the mould was used to make all shapes.

Constellation

Shown in a 1914 Butler Brothers ad for Dugan/Diamond Glass Company this very scarce compote was reported to be available in both white and blue opalescent. Originally the mould for this piece was the S-Repeat goblet (the pattern was originally called National and was a product of Northwood/National Glass that dated to 1903). When Dugan obtained the National moulds, the exterior pattern became S-Repeat and the goblet was turned into a compote with a pattern on the interior called Constellation. In addition to the few opalescent items, many shapes were made in colored crystal with gilding, as well as a few shapes in carnival glass including the compote where the S-Repeat exterior is known as Seafoam! Another example of name complication that plagues collectors.

Coral

Found only on bowls with odd open work around the edging, the Coral pattern may well be a product of the Jefferson Company. Colors are the usual: white, blue, green, and vaseline. And while it has the same name as a Fenton carnival glass pattern, the design is far different.

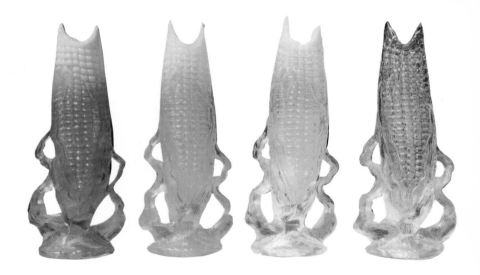

Corn Vase

Corn Vase

Despite having been reproduced by Wright Glass in the 1960s, this beautiful Dugan pattern is a collector's dream. Dugan made it in 1905 in white, blue, vaseline, and a rare green, as well as, a super-rare marigold carnival. The mould work is fantastic and the open husks show real glassmaking skill. Shown are blue, vaseline, white, and a rare stained crystal vase.

Cornucopia

This very attractive Northwood novelty vase dates to 1905, and can be found in white or blue opalescent glass. While it has been reported in carnival glass, I've never seen an example in my 26 years of collecting. The design is a nice one, almost like a basket weave that flares to handles on two sides while the rolled bottom rests on a decorative base.

Cornucopia

Curtain Optic

Fenton began making this very pretty design in 1922 and continued for several years, adding a medium wide striped opalescent pattern called Rib Optic. These patterns were made in several pitcher sizes and shapes along with iced tea tumblers, handled tall tumblers, and handled mugs. Even a two-piece guest set (small bedside pitcher and tumbler) can be found. Usually, the handles on both pitchers and mugs were of a darker glass. Some of these opalescent items were iridized.

Curtain Optic

25

Dahlia Twist

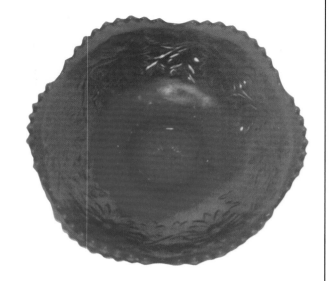

Daisy and Plume

*D*ahlia Twist

Made by the Jefferson Glass Company around 1905, Dahlia Twist was originally Jefferson's #207 pattern. It is a typical cone-shaped vase on a circular base with a flared and ruffled top. The real interest comes in the ribbing that is twisted against an interior optic that runs in the opposite direction. Colors are the typical white, green, and blue opalescent.

*D*aisy and Plume

While this famous design was made for years under the Northwood/National banner, the example shown comes from the Dugan Company, despite having no holes in the legs. The mould work is excellent and there is no Northwood marking. Colors are green, white, and blue opalescent glass and carnival glass. Dugan ads date from 1907 on this footed rose bowl.

*D*aisy Wreath

I am extremely pleased to show this very rare item from the Westmoreland company. It is usually found in carnival glass on a milk glass base, but here we have a rich blue glass with opalescent edges. The bowl is 9" in diameter and is the only example in opalescent glass I've seen without iridescence.

Daisy Wreath

Diamonds

Diamonds

Made by Hobbs, Brockunier & Company, this cute bud vase dates from 1888. In addition to being opalescent, it has an added coralene decoration of flowers and leaves in the tiny glass beading that was so popular at the time. Usually found on water pitchers (two shapes), in cranberry, this vase is a real rarity. It is only 5" tall.

Diamond and Daisy

Ads in a 1909 Butler Brothers catalog identify this pattern as part of the Intaglio line from the Dugan Company. It is clearly shown in a handled basket shape, so we know at least two shapes were made. Dugan first advertised the Intaglio line in 1905, and it included painted plain crystal as well as white opalescent. The pattern of Diamond and Daisy is very similar to the Wheel and Block pattern.

Diamond and Oval Thumbprint

This very attractive design, found only on the vase shape, is from the Jefferson Glass Company, circa 1904. It can be found in white, blue, or green opalescent glass and may vary in size from 6" tall to 14".

Diamond and Daisy

Diamond and Oval Thumbprint

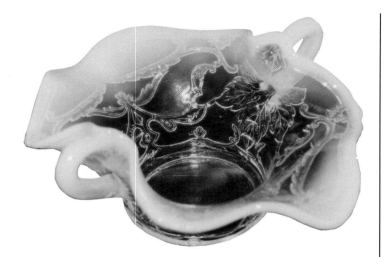

Diamond Maple Leaf

Diamond Optic

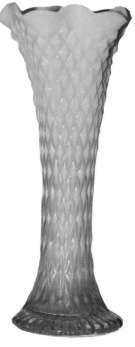

Diamond Point

Diamond Maple Leaf

Attributed to the Dugan Glass Company (Dugan/Diamond), this hard to find two-handled bon-bon can be found in green, white, and blue opalescent. The design shows rather realistic maple leaves flanked by very flowing scroll designs that give the piece a real artistic look. Diamond Maple Leaf dates from 1909.

Diamond Optic

I know very little about this attractive piece except it is from England. I base this on the finish and shaping. It may be known by another name also, but I felt this name summed up the configuration as well as any. The diamond pattern is all on the inside and runs from the outer rim to a middle diameter above the stem. It can be found in white opalescent also, and may well have been made in canary or vaseline.

Diamond Point

Found only on the vase shape, this Northwood pattern dates from 1907, and can be found in white, blue, and green opalescent glass and many carnival glass colors. Sizes range from 8" to a lofty 14" that has been swung to reach that size.

Diamond Point and Fleur de Lis

Since this pattern is shown in a 1906 Butler Brothers ad showing other Northwood patterns including Beaded Cable, a Diamond Point vase, Leaf and Beads, Spokes and Wheels, and Wild Rose, there is little doubt of the maker. In addition, it can occasionally be found with the Northwood trademark. Colors are white, blue, and green opalescent and the shapes are bowl novelties.

Diamond Point Columns

While many carnival glass collectors are familiar with this pattern and associate it with the Imperial Glass Company of Bellaire, Ohio, it was also a product of the Fenton Company and is shown in Butler Brothers ads with other Fenton patterns. In opalescent glass, only the vase has been reported and I am very happy to show an example of this rarity. This opalescent piece stands 12" tall and was made in 1907.

Diamond Spearhead

First produced by Northwood as part of the National Glass line (#22) as early as 1901, this very nice geometric pattern can be found in table sets, water sets, goblets, berry sets, a toothpick holder, mug, syrup, salt shaker, decanter, celery vase, tall (tankard) creamer, jelly compote, a tall (fruit) compote, and cup and saucer. Colors known are green, white, vaseline, blue, sapphire blue, and plain crystal glass.

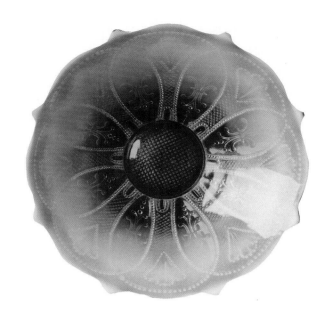

Diamond Point and Fleur de Lis

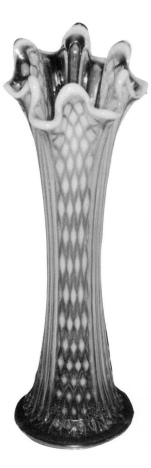

*Diamond Point
Columns*

Diamond Spearhead

Dolphin

Dolphin and Herons

Dolphin

Originally made by the Northwood Company as early as 1902, this beautiful compote has been widely reproduced in all colors, so buy only what you are confident with. Colors are white, blue, and vaseline. The older compotes have a stronger color and better glass clarity but those are about the only differences.

Dolphin and Herons

A product of the Model Flint Glass Company of Albany, Indiana, while a part of National, this hard-to-find novelty can be seen in both a compote shape or flattened into a stemmed tray. The stem is the dolphin, turning back on its tail, almost swallowing the bowl which has herons and fauna. Colors are white, blue, and canary in opalescent glass as well as crystal.

Double Greek Key

Made in Fostoria, Ohio, by the Nickel Plate Glass Company and then continued by U.S. Glass, this very attractive pattern dates to 1892. Shapes known are table sets, berry sets, water sets, a celery vase, toothpick holder, mustard pot, pickle dish, and salt shakers. Colors are white and blue opalescent, as well as plain crystal.

Double Greek Key

Double Stem Rose

Double Stem Rose

While this famous Dugan/Diamond pattern is very well-known in carnival glass, the example shown is the first in opalescent glass I've seen. It has to be quite rare. The pattern dates from 1910, and I'm sure this bowl was an early product. As you can see, it has the very typical Dugan one-two-one crimp and may well show up in other opalescent colors including blue and green, and each of these would be equally rare.

Drapery (Fenton)

While the Blown Drapery pattern was made at the Northwood Company, the Fenton example is mould-blown and dates to 1910, five years later than Northwood's. In addition, the Fenton version has a shorter, ball-shaped pitcher while the Northwood version is tankard shape. Fenton Drapery colors are the usual white, blue, and green opalescent with amethyst being a possibility.

Drapery (Northwood)

Sometimes called Northwood's Drapery, this interesting pattern dates from 1904, and usually is marked. Colors are white and blue opalescent, often with gold decorated edges and ribbing. Shapes known are table sets, water sets, berry sets, and some novelty items including a vase whimsey and a rose bowl. Some of the shapes were carried over into carnival glass production; these include rose bowls, candy dishes (from the same mould), and the vase shape.

Drapery (Fenton)

Drapery (Northwood)

Dugan's Daisy Intaglio

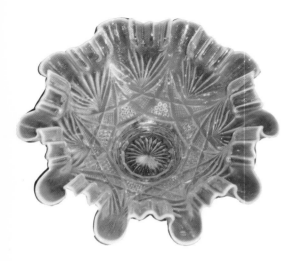

Dugan's Diamond Compass

Dugan Hexagon Base

Dugan's Daisy Intaglio

In 1905 the Dugan Glass Company began a line of crystal that was often opalescent, sometimes with goofus treatment. In addition, in a 1909 Butler Brothers ad, they advertised three designs in baskets, all part of this intaglio line. The example shown is the Daisy pattern, one of three designs that included Wilted Flowers and a pattern similar to Wheel and Block, but with Primroses added. In addition, I've seen this Daisy Intaglio pattern without the handle in a square bowl shape in green opalescent. I'm sure these pieces were made in other opalescent colors, too, including white and blue.

Dugan's Diamond Compass

I am very happy to be able to show the bridge that has caused so much confusion between Reflecting Diamonds and Compass, both patterns by the Dugan/Diamond Company. If you will take time to examine all three of these patterns closely, you will see the marie (base) pattern on Diamond Compass is totally different than either of the other patterns. In addition there are differences in the arc interior designs. I'm sure this very surprising pattern will show up in blue, but green and white are the only ones I've heard about. Note the dome base.

Dugan Hexagon Base

This very pretty Dugan vase with the hex base and the jack-in-the-pulpit turned top, stands 7½" tall. The coloring is very good and the mould work excellent. I suspect this vase was made in white and possibly green opalescent, and perhaps with a ruffled top. It dates from the 1907 – 1910 period..

Dugan Intaglio

Designed in 1904 for a line of mostly goofus ware, Dugan's Intaglio designs were primarily fruit patterns (very rare examples of flowers and birds exist) that had a gold and colored treatment to the leaves and fruits while the rest of the glass remained crystal. Fruits found are cherries, grapes, strawberries, and plums, while flower patterns were mostly roses and poppies. Not all of these pieces had opalescence but a few did; we are showing a very pretty Cherries bowl which had red fruit and gilt leaves.

Dugan's Junior (Jack-in-the-Pulpit Vase)

If you will compare this Dugan vase to the stemmed Dugan Jack-in-the-Pulpit shown elsewhere you will see both have a wide ribbed exterior and are shaped exactly the same. This one is flat-based and measures 4½" tall while the hex-based one measures 7½" tall. The Junior is known in the usual opalescent colors of white, blue, and green.

Estate

Shown in a 1906 Butler Brothers catalog with other Dugan patterns, this unusual 4½" vase was advertised in white, blue, and green opalescent glass. These do not have the normal stippling associated with the carnival glass version and perhaps we should really call it Dugan Estate to separate it from the Westmoreland Estate pattern that is similar. At any rate, the Dugan Estate piece should be considered a real find in opalescent glass for they are quite scarce in any color.

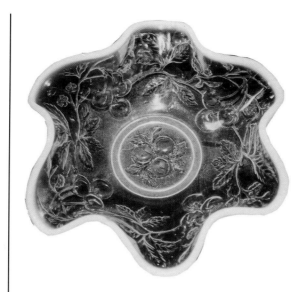

Dugan Intaglio

Dugan's Junior

Estate

Everglades

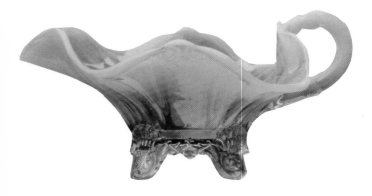

Fan

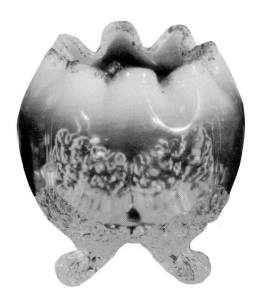

Fancy Fantails

*E*verglades
Originally called Carnelian, this Northwood pattern dates from 1903. It was made in several treatments beside opalescent glass including custard and purple slag. Opalescent colors are white, blue, and canary, with some limited production in green. Shapes made are table sets, water sets, berry sets that are oval in shape, cruets, salt shakers, and jelly compotes. Note that the items shown all have a decorative gilding on the design and the floral sprays, and the vaseline coloring shows a good deal of green.

*F*an
Long considered a Northwood pattern, Fan is actually from the Dugan/Diamond plant, shown in a 1907 company ad in water sets, berry sets, and table sets in ivory (custard) and opalescent glass in colors of green, white, and blue. In a whimsey plate that was shaped from the spooner, the glass almost glows with opalescence. Fan was also made in emerald green and cobalt blue, sometimes with gold decoration, as well as, limited shapes in carnival glass.

*F*ancy Fantails
While others credit this pattern to the Northwood Company, I'm convinced it is from Jefferson. As I've said before, research has convinced me most (if not all) of the cranberry decorated items came from Jefferson Glass. Fancy Fantails dates from 1905, and can be found in both rose bowls and candy dishes from the same mould. Colors are white, blue, green, and vaseline.

Fenton's #220 Stripe

Feathers

No question about the maker of this vase since most are marked with the Northwood trademark. Vases are the only shape, and the colors are white, blue, and green opalescent, as well as, carnival glass colors. Sizes range from 7" to a pulled 13". I've seen a blue opalescent and a white opalescent vase with gold edging.

Fenton's #220 Stripe

Found in iced tea sets (both pitcher and tumblers have contrasting colored handles) and nights sets (tumble-ups), this was a popular Fenton pattern, produced in 1929. Colors are blue, green, white, and vaseline, and there are two shapes and sizes in pitchers. Note that the one shown has a matching lid but not all shapes do.

Fenton's #370

This beauty dates from the 1924 – 1927 period of Fenton production. The cameo opalescent coloring is a real treat and I'm happy to be able to show this example. This same coloring can be found in many patterns and shapes in the Fenton line including bowls, vases, nappies, and bon-bons. The base color of the glass is a strong amber and the opalescence is a rich creamy tint.

Feathers   *Fenton's #370*

Fenton's Vintage

Finecut and Roses

Fish-in-the-Sea

Fenton's Vintage (Leaf)

Seen mostly in carnival glass, this very distinct Fenton pattern dates from 1909 – 10 and can be recognized by its large leaf center as well as the five bunches of grapes that are grouped around the bowl. The exterior is plain, as is the marie. Colors reported are white, blue, and a rare amethyst. All colors are hard to find and well worth the search.

Finecut and Roses

Early opalescent production of this pattern was at Jefferson's Steubenville plant, however Northwood later produced this pattern in their lines of custard and carnival glass. Colors in opalescent glass are white, blue, and green. Shapes (all from the same mould) are footed candy dishes, rose bowls, and a shape called a spooner that is slightly ruffled.

Fish-in-the-Sea

There is a good bit of doubt about the origin of this very strong pattern but both Northwood and Dugan/Diamond are strong possibilities. It has been found with some goofus decoration which both companies used, but it has a European look. Colors are white, blue, and green. This vase is a scarce item, much sought by collectors.

Flora

Flora

Dating from 1898 this Beaumont pattern can be found in a host of shapes including table sets, water sets, berry sets, shakers, cruets, syrups, toothpick holders, compotes, celery vases, and several bowl novelty shapes. Colors are blue, white, and vaseline with some items gilded. Other types of glass were also made in Flora including crystal and emerald green, which can also be found with gilding.

Floral Eyelet

Little is known about this very scarce pattern; it is believed to be a product of Northwood/National or even Dugan at the Indiana, Pennsylvania, plant. The time of production has been speculated from 1896 to 1905 with the only shapes being a water pitcher and tumbler in white, blue, and cranberry opalescent. The tumbler is shown here. The reproduced pitcher, made by the L.G. Wright Company, is shown elsewhere in this book. The new pitchers have reeded handles while the old do not.

Floral Eyelet

Fluted Bars and Beads

While previous writers have credited this very interesting pattern to the Northwood Company, I am convinced it is a Jefferson Glass Company product, dating to 1905 or 1906. The colors in opalescent glass are white, blue, green, and vaseline, often with a cranberry edging (a reason to suggest Jefferson as the maker). The design is a simple one of two sections of threading and beads that border a center area of fluting.

Fluted Bars and Beads

Fluted Scrolls

*Fluted Scrolls
with Vine*

Gonterman Swirl

Fluted Scrolls (Jackson)

Originally called Klondyke, this multi-titled pattern is known today as either Fluted Scrolls or Jackson. It was first advertised in 1898 by the Northwood Company and can be found in table sets, water sets, berry sets, cruets, salt shakers, a puff box (also called "baby butter"), two-piece epergne, and various bowl shapes. Colors are blue, white, and vaseline opalescent as well as custard, green, and crystal glass. Sometimes this pattern is decorated, giving rise to still another name, Fluted Scrolls with Flower Band.

Fluted Scrolls with Vine

Shown as early as 1899 in a Butler Brothers ad, this Northwood Glass Company pattern is one of my favorite vase designs. It is known in white, blue, and canary and may also show up in green one of these days. I am constantly amazed at the colors and patterns that have been overlooked for years. The design of flowers, stems, and leaves winding around a fluted, cone-shaped vase is very pretty when you add the base of spread leaves and the top rim of scalloped blossoms, the whole piece becomes a real work of art.

Gonterman Swirl

Attributed to Hobbs, Brockunier & Company of Wheeling, this very attractive pattern dates to 1886, and can be found in table sets, water sets, berry sets, cruet, syrup, celery vase, lamp shade, and a toothpick holder (sometimes in a metal frame). Pieces can be found with a blue or amber top edge while the base can be opalescent or frosted. While some items are signed "Patented August 4, 1876," this is not the date of production and probably refers to a design patent by Louis Wagner covering the fusing process used to create this pattern.

Grape and Cable

I feel very privileged to show this quite rare example of this Northwood pattern, since so very few examples of any shape are found in opalescent glass, only the large centerpiece footed bowl (mislabeled as a punch bowl in some books) in white and this stunning handled bon-bon in vaseline opalescent with a strong greenish cast. In carnival glass and custard this pattern proved to be one of Northwood's best and literally dozens of shapes exist. Please note the bon-bon carries a second well-known Northwood pattern called Basketweave.

Grape and Cherry

While most writers list this nice bowl pattern as being from an unknown maker, I'm convinced it is a pattern that was made by the Sowerby Glass Works of England. I base this on years of experience with carnival glass from both American and foreign makers; Grape and Cherry in carnival glass has frequently been associated with British production. In opalescent glass, it is found in white and blue only, another hint of English origin. At any rate, it is a nice pattern with alternating ovals of grapes and cherries with a neat scrolling and torch design separating the sections.

Grapevine Cluster

Every time I see one of these imaginative vase patterns from the opalescent age, I am amazed by the artistic abilities in their design. Grapevine cluster is another Northwood pattern, dating from 1905. It has a grape leaf base, twig supporting branches, and realistic grapes in a cluster. Colors are the usual white, blue, and vaseline or canary but it can also be found in non-opalescent purple slag from the Mosaic line.

Grape and Cable

Grape and Cherry

Grapevine Cluster

39

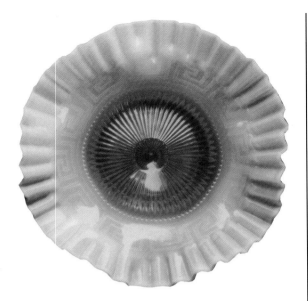

Greek Key and Ribs

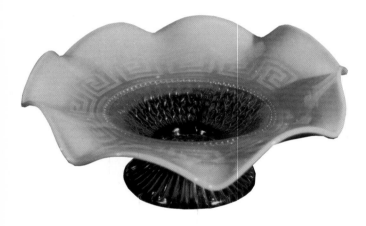

Greek Key and Scales

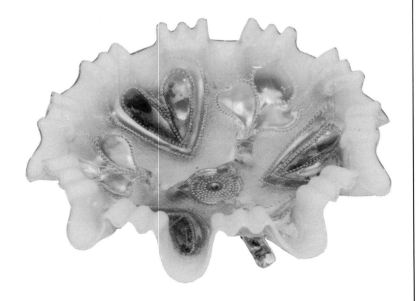

Hearts and Clubs

Greek Key and Ribs

This Northwood bowl pattern is similar to the Greek Key and Scales bowl shown below. Dating from the 1907 production, the dome based bowl can be found in white, blue, green, and canary, as well as the host of carnival colors. Just why one company would create two moulds so similar is a mystery but it seemed to happen frequently, especially in opalescent and carnival glass. Perhaps competition forced so many variations but I can't be sure. At any rate, it makes collecting more interesting for all of us.

Greek Key and Scales

Made by the Northwood Company in 1905, this often marked pattern is well-known in both opalescent glass and carnival. The bowl shape has a dome base and is usually ruffled. Opalescent colors are white, green, and blue.

Hearts and Clubs

This Jefferson Glass Company pattern was originally their #274 and was produced about 1905. As you can see the footed bowl shown here has a goofus treatment, but it can be found on blue and green opalescent glass as well. The three feet of the bowl are shaped like those on the Daisy and Plume pieces made by Northwood and later Dugan, but are solid without any portholes.

Hearts and Flowers

This well-known Northwood pattern can be found in carnival, custard, and opalescent glass. In the latter, it is seen on compotes and bowls in white, blue, and very rarely vaseline. Production dates from 1908, when the maker added several well-known patterns to their opalescent production on a limited basis, including Singing Birds, Peacock on the Fence, Rose Show, Grape and Cable, Three Fruits, Bushel Basket, Acorn Burrs, Beaded Cable, Finecut and Roses, and Daisy and Plume. All were made mainly in white or blue, with a few vaseline items.

Hearts and Flowers

Heart Handled Open O's

While this is primarily the same pattern as the Open O's we show elsewhere, the handled ring basket has always been shown on its own and we will keep it that way. It is a Northwood pattern, dating from 1905 – 06. Colors are white, blue, and green, with canary a strong possibility.

Heron and Peacock

While I have very little information about this child's mug, known as Heron and Peacock, I believe it to be an old example. I've been told it has been made in many glass treatments over the years and is listed in one book on children's collectibles as having once been made in crystal and cobalt blue, but this is the first I've actually seen. It may well have been made in other opalescent colors and a blue or canary one would be outstanding. The design has a peacock on one side and the heron on the other with floral sprays dividing them. The opalescence is quite good. It is currently being reproduced by Boyd Crystal Art Glass, Cambridge, Ohio.

Heart Handled Open O's

Heron and Peacock

Herringbone (Plain)

Herringbone (Ribbed)

Hilltop Vines

Herringbone (Plain)

Since shards of this pattern were found at the Indiana, PA, plant, we can be confident one of the makers of Herringbone (both plain and ribbed) was the Northwood Glass Company. Shard colors were white, yellow, and blue, but of course, cranberry items are also known. Items known are water sets, cruets, syrups, and crimped salad bowls. Some treatments are cased mother-of-pearl in a satin finish. The plain Herringbone dates to 1885, when Harry Northwood was at the Phoenix Glass concern.

Herringbone (Ribbed)

As I said in the narrative about plain Herringbone, this is most likely a Northwood pattern, found on water sets, cruets, syrups, and crimped salad bowls in white, blue, cranberry, and canary opalescent glass. While the plain Herringbone came first and dates to Northwood's days at Phoenix, the ribbed Herringbone is believed to date to about 1902, at the Indiana, PA, plant. Since I felt the two treatments were so different, I believe they should be discussed as separate items.

Hilltop Vines

This unusual compote is shown in Northwood ads as early as 1906, so we know who made it. It can be found in white, blue, and green opalescent glass and stands roughly 5" tall. Outstanding features are the leaves that overlap, making up the bowl of the compote, the branch-like legs that form the stem, and the domed base covered with tiny bubble-like circles.

Hobnail (Hobbs)

Here is the Hobnail salt shaker from Hobbs, Brockunier, unreported until recently. Other shapes made in this well-known pattern are water sets, table sets, berry sets (square shaped), cruets, syrups, finger bowls, celery vase, barber bottle, water tray, bride's basket with frame, and five sizes of pitchers. Production of the Hobbs Hobnail design began in 1885 and lasted until 1892. Colors reported are white, blue, rubina, vaseline, and cranberry.

Hobnail

Hobnail-in-Square (Vesta)

Made by the Aetna Glass & Mfg. Company of Bellaire, Ohio, the Hobnail-in-Square pattern was originally called Vesta and dates from circa 1887. It has been reproduced in recent years, particularly by Fenton in the 1950s and for A & A, an import house, in the mid-1970s. Reproduced shapes include vases, epergnes, and small odd pieces. In the old items, shapes are water sets, table sets, berry sets, a celery vase, salt shakers, and a variety of compotes including the very beautiful one shown on a nice metal stand. Colors are mostly white opalescent but here is a rare blue piece. Vesta was also made in crystal.

Hobnail-in-Square

Honeycomb and Clover

Made by the Fenton Company in several types of glass including carnival, opalescent, and gilt decorated. Production in opalescent glass dates from 1910, and the colors known are the usual white, blue, and green. However, amethyst is a definite possibility and would be a real find. The pattern is exterior and consists of an all-over honeycombing with clover and leaves twining over it. Shapes in opalescent glass are water sets, berry sets, table sets, and novelty bowls.

Honeycomb and Clover

Idyll

Intaglio

Interior Panel

Idyll

Made by Jefferson Glass, Idyll can be found in water sets, table sets, berry sets, a toothpick holder, cruet and salt shakers sometimes grouped on a tray, and an intermediate size bowl. Colors in opalescent glass are blue, green, and white, and the pattern can also be found in crystal, gilded green, and blue. Idyll dates from 1907.

Intaglio

One of Northwood's earlier patterns, dating from 1897, in custard production, Intaglio was made in a host of shapes including table sets, water sets, berry sets, a cruet, salt shakers, a jelly compote, and many novelty shapes. Colors made in opalescent glass are white, blue, and occasionally canary, but other treatments such as gilded emerald green and, of course, custard are available.

Interior Panel

This very nice Fenton vase dates from the early 1920s and besides the fine example in amber opalescent, I've seen it in Cameo opalescent, iridized stretch glass in Celeste Blue, Velva Rose, and Florentine Green; all from the 1921 – 1927 era of production. The same mould was used to make a trumpet vase also. The example shown is 8" tall and has a fan spread of 5".

Interior Swirl

Interior Swirl

Much like the Inside Ribbing pattern but with a twist, this very pretty rose bowl is perfectly plain on the outside and has a ribbing that has been twisted on the interior. Notice the cranberry frett along the top indicating this pattern is most likely from Jefferson Glass. One writer dates this pattern to the 1890s but I'd place it closer to 1904 or 1905. The canary coloring is quite good and the base prominent.

Inverted Fan and Feather

Certainly one of Northwood's better patterns, Inverted Fan and Feather can be found on water sets, table sets, berry sets, jelly compotes, punch bowl, punch cups, toothpick holder, salt shaker, a rare cruet, and whimseys that include a spittoon shape. Opalescent colors are white, blue, and canary, often with gilding but the pattern can also be found in custard, gilded emerald green, and carnival glass. First made in 1904, production continued for several more years.

Inverted Fan and Feather

Iris with Meander

Iris with Meander is also known as Fleur-de-Lis Scrolled and is a product of Jefferson Glass, dating to 1902 or 1903. It was made in table sets, water sets, berry sets (two sizes of sauces), toothpick holder, salt shaker, jelly compote, vase, pickle dish, and the plate shown. Colors are flint, blue, canary, green, and rarely amber opalescent, as well as crystal, blue, green, and amethyst glass with decoration.

Iris with Meander

Jackson

Jefferson Shield

Jefferson Spool

Jackson

May I say I personally hate not calling this pattern and Fluted Scrolls by the original name that covered both patterns, Klondyke, but I will bow to previous writers. Jackson is a Northwood pattern and can be found on table sets, water sets, berry sets, cruets, candy dishes, and a mini-epergne. Colors are white, blue, canary, and limited amounts of green. It was also made in custard glass.

Jefferson Shield

This very rare pattern was from the Jefferson Glass Company, produced as their #262 pattern. It is a dome-based bowl, found in green, white, and blue opalescent. It has a series of 13 shields around the center of the bowl. If you are the owner of one of these bowls, consider yourself very lucky, for less than one dozen in all colors are known!

Jefferson Spool

This very unusual vase by the Jefferson Glass Company looks as if it were turned on a lathe. It stands approximately 8" tall and was made in 1905. Colors reported in opalescent glass are white, green, blue, and vaseline. No other shapes have been seen, but it could easily have been opened into a compote.

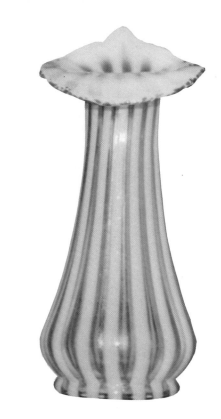

Jefferson Stripe

Jefferson Stripe

This very pretty Jack-in-the-Pulpit vase in opalescent Stripe has a pretty cranberry edging that is a giveaway to its maker — the Jefferson Company. It has a collar base and stands 8½" tall. As you can see, the coloring is almost an emerald green and the opalescent striping goes all the way down the base. It was made in white and blue.

Jefferson Wheel

This very attractive bowl dating from 1905 is, as the name implies, another pattern from Jefferson Glass. It was originally Jefferson's #260 pattern and can be found in white, blue, or green opalescent glass. It has been reported in carnival, but I seriously doubt that possibility.

Jewels and Drapery

This very pretty Northwood vase dates to 1907, and can be found in ads from that year. As you can see, the drapery is very well done with a tiny tassel ending between the folds. Around the base are a series of jewels or raised dots. Strangely, in a Northwood ad in a 1906 Lyons Brothers catalog, there is a similar vase shown that has an additional row of pendants below the jewels. The ad is labeled the Fairmont opal assortment. To date I haven't seen any examples of this vase.

Jewels and Drapery

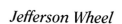

Jefferson Wheel

Jewel and Fan

Jewel and Fan

Jefferson made a lot of opalescent glass and here is still another pattern which was originally identified as their #125. It is found on bowls and an elongated banana bowl in white, blue, green, and rarely canary. The design is simple but very effective.

Jewel and Flower

Made by the Northwood Company in 1904, and originally called Encore, this very attractive pattern can be found on water sets, table sets, berry sets, cruets, and salt shakers. Colors are white, blue, and canary, often decorated with gilding as in the example shown. Incidentally, there is a variant with the design going all the way to the base and eliminating the beading and threading band.

Jewelled Heart

Long credited to Northwood, Jewelled Heart (or Victor, as it was originally called) was first made by Dugan in 1905. Shapes available are table sets, water sets, berry sets, a syrup, sugar shaker, a condiment set consisting of cruet, salt and pepper shakers, and toothpick holder on a round flat tray or plate. Colors in opalescent glass are white, green, and blue, but the pattern is also found in carnival glass, crystal, green, and blue decorated glass, and very rarely ivory or custard glass. Some items are marked with the Diamond-D marking.

Jewel and Flower

Jewelled Heart

Jolly Bear

Credited to the Northwood Glass Company (I'm still a skeptic), this pattern was made in the 1906 – 08 era. It is reported in white, blue, and green opalescent, sometimes with gilding; however, I've only seen it in the white. The example shown exhibits a good deal of the gold goofus work. There is a carnival glass pattern in very scarce water set pieces called Frolicking Bears which looks a good deal like the Jolly Bear bowl. Frolicking Bear is from the U.S. Glass Company, not Northwood.

Keyhole

Also shown in 1905 Dugan Glass Company ads is the Keyhole pattern. It can be found in opalescent glass on bowls that have a dome base in white, blue, and green; and painted or goofus treatment on the white. A few years later, it was adapted for use as the exterior of carnival glass bowls with Raindrop pattern as an interior and on a very rare marigold bowl where the exterior is plain and Keyhole became the interior pattern.

Lady Caroline

Another Davison pattern, this very cute English item was one believed to be made only in blue opalescent, but as you can see, a very pretty canary item is shown. Shapes known are baskets, a breakfast set consisting of creamer and sugar, and the neat little three-handled whimsey shown. No larger table set items have been reported and no pieces with the Rd number usually found on British glass. The pattern dates from 1891, when it was advertised as Patent Blue Pearline (apparently when blue was the only color!).

Jolly Bear

Keyhole

Lady Caroline

49

Late Coinspot

Lattice and Daisy

Lattice Medallions

Opalescent
Glass,
1880 – 1930

Late Coinspot

Here is a Fenton version of the famed Coinspot. This one dating from the 1925 – 29 era was called an iced tea set in advertising, and had a taller tumbler with it. Colors were white, blue, and green. As you can easily see, it has a semi-cannonball shape and the handle is rather thick. In 1931 Fenton made this same pitcher with a dark, contrasting handle, and teamed it with mugs with the same handle treatment.

Lattice and Daisy

Shown in a Butler Brothers ad in 1914 that features several Dugan Glass patterns in opalescent glass, the Lattice and Daisy tumbler was apparently the only shape in this pattern offered in this type of glass. In carnival glass, the complete water set, as well as a berry set, are shown. The opalescent colors listed in the ad for this tumbler were white and blue, but as you can see, a very rare vaseline was made. Strangely, the iridized glass production of this pattern was also 1914, so it may just be that the opalescent pieces were made to fill the packing amounts needed for shipment, since all items in the opalescent ad are considered quite scarce. They include the Mary Ann vase, the Windflower bowl, the Stork and Rushes mug, the Constellation compote, and Fishscale and Beads items.

Lattice Medallions

This very graceful pattern is from the Northwood Company and is sometimes marked with the famous "N." Found primarily in bowl shapes, often very ruffled and ornately shaped, Lattice Medallions can be found in the usual opalescent colors of white, blue, and green. Shown is a very pretty white opalescent bowl with the tri-corner shaping.

Lattice and Points

*L*attice and Points

This Dugan pattern is pulled from the same mould that producing the Vining Twigs plates and bowls that were made in carnival glass (as were the vases). In opalescent glass, the vases are usually short and haven't been pulled or swung as most vases are. Colors are white, mostly, but scarce blue examples are known and I suspect green was made also. Production of the opalescent pieces date from 1907.

*L*aura (Single Flower Framed)

Here is another example of poor naming; the Laura name is from Rose Presznick but the pattern has long been called Single Flower Framed by carnival glass collectors. It is a Dugan pattern, found only on the exterior of nappies, bowls, and this very rare ruffled plate. Colors previously reported are white and blue opalescent, as well as carnival colors (especially peach opalescent), but as you can see, this plate is in a very pretty green opalescent. These scarce items date from the 1909 period of Dugan production.

Laura

*L*eaf and Beads

Just why Northwood decided to make these bowls with both a dome base and the more familiar three twig feet is a mystery, but both can be found with the trademark (not all are marked). Production began in 1905 and by 1906 both shapes were appearing in ads. Colors in opalescent glass are white, blue, and green. Leaf and Beads was also made in custard glass and carried over into carnival glass.

Leaf and Beads

51

Leaf and Diamonds

Leaf and Leaflets

Leaf and Diamonds

Here is another Dugan/Diamond pattern that can occasionally be found with a goofus finish. The bowl measures 9" across and has the typical Dugan 3-1-3 edge scalloping. There are three large spatula feet. It can be found in white, blue, and occasionally green. Strangely, the pattern is almost a companion to the Hearts and Clubs pattern made by Jefferson.

Leaf and Leaflets

Here is another of those patterns that appeared first in Northwood's lineup (1907 ads) and later became part of the Dugan production line. The opalescent examples in blue, white, and goofus are Northwood, however the same mould turns up later as a Dugan carnival glass pattern called Long Leaf in a beautiful peach opalescent iridized bowl. In addition, Long Leaf can be found as the exterior design for bowls and baskets of the Stippled Petals design in peach opalescent, also made by Dugan!

Leaf Chalice

Made by Northwood while a part of the National combine, Leaf Chalice appears in a May, 1903, Butler Brothers ad that featured three shapings of the piece. Colors usually found are white or blue, but green was also made as you can see and is considered a rare color in this pattern.

Leaf Chalice

Lined Heart

Lined Heart

Dating from 1906, this Jefferson Glass Company vase pattern can be found in white, blue, and green opalescent glass. The examples shown haven't been swung as many are and are about 7" tall; some range to 14" however.

Lion Store Souvenir (Beaded Stars Advertising)

Why so very few of these Fenton advertising pieces exist or why there are so very few advertising items in all of opalescent glass is a real mystery. The only pieces reported in Beaded Stars are one bowl and two plates. They read: SOUVENIR LION STORE HAMMOND. All three items are in blue.

Little Nell

Despite being very plain, this vase is still a very cute item. Except for the threading above the collar base, there is no design at all and whatever the vase has going for it comes from the shaping and fine opalescence. The maker isn't certain at this time and I'm not sure it really matters. Colors are white, blue, and green opalescent.

Lion Store Souvenir

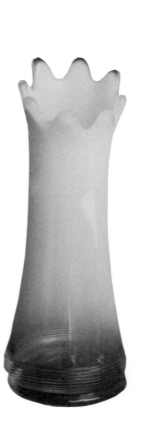

Little Nell

Little Swan (Dugan)

Little Swan (Northwood)

Lorna

*L*ittle Swan (Dugan)

Slightly larger than the Northwood swan shown below, the Dugan version came along in 1909, and can be found in white, green, and blue opalescent glass and various carnival glass colors. The Fenton Company also made a version, but the breast feathering is quite different from the two versions here — more like flower petals than feathers.

*L*ittle Swan (Northwood)

Virtually the same design as the Dugan Little Swan, the Northwood version came first and is slightly smaller. It can be found in blue and white (green may be a possibility but I've only seen Dugan ones in that color). Some examples have been gilded on the head and along the rim of the opening and down the tail.

*L*orna

Credited first to the Model Flint Glass Company of Albany, Indiana, Northwood nevertheless shows this vase as #562 in a 1900 ad. Obviously, since shards were found in Albany, this vase was copied. At any rate, it is found in white, blue, and canary opalescent glass and stands about 6½" tall.

Lustre Flute

Lustre Flute

Another Northwood product, Lustre Flute can be found in water sets, table sets, berry sets, custard cups, and vases in opalescent colors of white or blue. The pattern was later made in carnival colors that date to the 1912 era but the vast opalescent production dates to 1907 – 08. Shown is an example with gilt decoration. Lustre Flute is also known as Waffle Band and English Hob Band, but the Lustre Flute title is most widely used.

Many Loops

Many Loops was Jefferson's #247 pattern. It is found only on bowls and in the usual opalescent colors of white, blue, and green. The design of overlapping loops, while busy, is very pleasant and reminds one of the child's drawing game Spirograph.

Many Ribs

This very distinctive vase with a columnal base was made by the Model Flint Glass Company of Albany, Indiana, in 1902. It can be found in white, blue, and the very attractive canary shown. This particular vase measures nearly 8" and has the typical slightly flared top.

Many Loops

Many Ribs

Maple Leaf

Maple Leaf Chalice

Mary Ann

Maple Leaf

Apparently first a Northwood pattern (at least in custard glass), the opalescent items and later carnival glass production were definitely Dugan products. The opalescent glass dates from 1908 – 10. Colors in this glass are green (scarce), white, and blue with a very rare example in vaseline shown. The only shape reported in opalescent glass seems to be the jelly compote, but others may certainly exist.

Maple Leaf Chalice

Another one of the naturalistic pieces from the Northwood Company made in purple slag, as well as opalescent glass. This very pretty vase dates from the 1903 – 05 era. Opalescent colors are white, blue, green, and vaseline. The design is much like Leaf Chalice, also from Northwood and the two are often confused.

Mary Ann

While this vase is well known to carnival glass collectors, it comes as a surprise to many who collect opalescent glass. It came from the Dugan Company, and received its name from the sister of Thomas E.A. and Alfred Dugan (Fanny Mary Ann Dugan). In carnival, the vase is known in an eight scallop and ten scallop top and a three handled, flat topped example called a loving cup. Carnival colors are marigold, amethyst, and a lighter lavender shade. There is also an amber glass example in satin finish. In opalescent glass, the only colors reported are white and blue and both are considered rare.

May Basket

May Basket

Still another Jefferson pattern, dating from 1906, this very attractive handled basket was their #87. It can be found in white, blue, and green opalescent glass. Interestingly enough, it has the exact same design as the Northwood Pump and Trough! Since Northwood production of this novelty set predates the Jefferson basket, the mind has to flinch at the obvious pirating that must have gone on.

Meander

Originally a Jefferson pattern (#233), the moulds were obtained by the Northwood Company after its move to the Wheeling location. The opalescent pieces in white, blue, and green are attributed to Jefferson, and the carnival bowls with Three Fruits Medallion as an interior pattern are strictly Northwood.

Meander

Melon Optic Swirl (Jefferson)

This very beautiful, tightly crimped bowl has a melon rib exterior that has been shaped into a swirl with a cranberry edging. The color is a fine vaseline. This bowl appears to be quite close to a series of pieces shown in a 1902 Jefferson ad, showing Stripe, Swirl, and Coindot items. The ad lists colors of white, blue, green, yellow (vaseline), and cranberry.

Melon Optic Swirl

Melon Swirl

Milky Way

Netted Roses

Melon Swirl

Having done a great deal of research and soul-searching, I'm convinced this very beautiful water set may well be from the Indiana, PA, plant at the time of early Dugan production. Examples of handles just like the one on the water set shown are found in 1904 ads showing decorated sets. In addition, the enamel work is so very similar to that found on several Dugan sets made between 1900 and 1905. These sets, more elaborate than most in this enameling, are consistent with Melon Swirl. I certainly hope someone out there can shed more light on this fantastic pattern. It is one of the prettiest I've ever seen.

Milky Way

To opalescent glass collectors this very rare Millersburg item (their only pattern in opalescent glass) is known as Milky Way, but to carnival glass collectors and especially those who collect Millersburg glass, this is a pattern known as Country Kitchen Variant. The only shape known is the small bowl and the example shown has been pulled into a square shape that measures 4"x6".

Netted Roses

Made by the Northwood Company in 1906, this bowl pattern is another of those with one name for opalescent glass and another for carnival. In carnival, the pattern is called Bullseye and Leaves, and is an exterior pattern also. In opalescent glass as Netted Roses, the colors are blue, green, and white, often with a goofus treatment as shown.

Northern Star

Another Fenton pattern, dating to 1908, this very nice geometric is most often found in carnival glass or crystal, but can rarely be found in large plates in white, blue, or green opalescent glass. Just why the small bowls and plates were not made in opalescent treatment is a mystery since 5" bowls, 7" plates, and 11" plates are all known in crystal.

Northwood Basket (Bushel Basket)

Sometimes trademarked, this Northwood novelty was made in limited amounts of opalescent glass in 1905 in white, vaseline, or blue. It was later made in large amounts of custard and carnival glass in many colors and even some shaping variations. The scarce blue opalescent example shown is marked and bears traces of gold paint in the creases of the handle design.

Northwood Block

While I bow to tradition with the name of this pattern, I loudly declare "I do not for one minute believe this is a Northwood pattern!" As you can see by the example shown, the top has the cranberry fritting that was so widely used by the Jefferson Glass Company, and as I said elsewhere in this book, I'm convinced all or nearly all of these pieces with this cranberry treatment are Jefferson. Having said that, the colors available for this Block pattern are white, blue, green, and canary. The only shapes are from one mould; either vase shapes or flattened into footed bowls. This pattern dates from 1905 – 09.

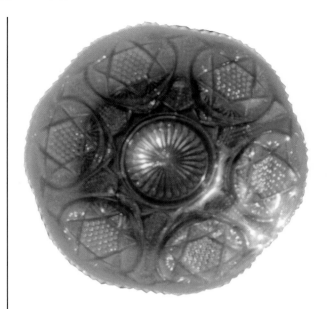

Northern Star

Northwood Basket

Northwood Block

Northwood Hobnail

Northwood's Many Ribs

Northwood's Shell

Northwood Hobnail

Dating from 1903 this hobnail pattern with the crimped standing rim can be found in table sets, water sets, berry sets, a mug, celery vase, and individual creamer and sugar. The only color reported is white but others may certainly have been made.

Northwood's Many Ribs

Unlike the Model Flint Glass example with this name, the base of the Northwood pattern is not columnated and the design just rolls to an even finish above the straight base. Colors are white, blue, green, and vaseline, and the vases range from 9" to 13" in size.

Northwood's Shell (Cleopatra)

Known in white, blue, and green opalescent glass, this very pretty vase is often mistaken for the Leaf Chalice vase or the Beaded Shell pattern which are both Dugan products. Actually, I know of no proof this vase is Northwood's but current "experts" place it in their production and there it will stay until proven to the contrary.

Northwood/Dugan Stripe

I'm told this vase came from the Indiana, PA, plant where both Northwood and Dugan/Diamond items in opalescent glass were made. As you can see, it is a very pretty canary Stripe and is shaped much like a vase in striped opalescent glass in an 1899 Northwood ad in a Butler Brothers catalog. I imagine it was produced in both white and blue also. It is about 7½" tall, with a collar base.

Ocean Shell

Still another of the naturalistic compotes with twig-like supports for stems, Ocean Shell has three variations of these. Some go all the way to the bowl, others are short and are not connected, while still others are longer but remain unattached at the top. Ocean Shell was made by Northwood Company, circa 1904. Opalescent colors are white, blue, and green, and purple slag glass is also known.

Old Man Winter

Shown in the two sizes made (the larger one is footed), this pattern came from the Jefferson Company and was advertised as their #135 (small) and #91 (large). The larger one is marked "Patent 1906" and a few of the smaller ones are marked "Patent March 18, 1902." I've seen the small baskets in white, blue, and green, but only in white and blue in the larger size. The very interesting handle treatment is a design giveaway and harkens back to Victorian baskets with decorative handles.

Northwood/Dugan Stripe

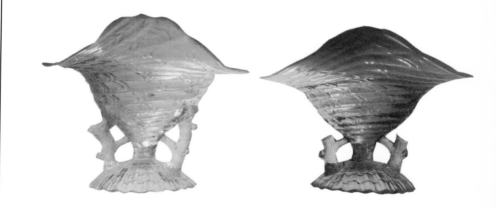

Ocean Shell

Old Man Winter

Opal Open

Open Edge Basketweave Base

*O*pal Open (Beaded Panels)

Carnival glass collectors have long known this pattern as Beaded Panels. Opalescent glass collectors call it Opal Open. It is shown in a Northwood ad in 1899, so we know they made it. But it later shows up in Dugan ads after 1907, and we know the iridized items are Dugan. To add to the complication, Westmoreland made a reproduction in the 1940s and 1950s that has a solid stem rather than pierced like the originals. Old pieces in opalescent glass were made in white, green, blue, and canary.

*O*pen Edge Basketweave Base

Introduced into the Fenton line in 1910, this novelty item has been a part of Fenton's production throughout the years, being made in opalescent glass, carnival glass, stretch glass, milk glass, opaque, and all sorts of clear colors. Shapes are bowls of three sizes, plates, candle holders, and vase whimseys. Carnival items sometimes have interior patterns. Early opalescent production colors are white, blue, green, and canary, but later production offered cobalt or royal blue and emerald green. These later examples date to the 1930s.

*O*pen O's

Advertised by Northwood as early as 1903, this very unusual pattern is known mostly in short, squat vase shapes, but it was also made in novelty bowls and a handled ring bowl. Colors are white, blue, green, and canary. It is possible Dugan continued production of this pattern once Northwood moved to Wheeling but, I can't confirm this at this time. The ring bowl is known as Heart Handled Open O's.

Open O's

Over-All Hobnail

Over-All Hobnail

First credited to Nickel Plate Glass, there is some reason to believe production continued once U.S. Glass acquired the plant in 1892. The Over-All Hobnail can be identified on most shapes by the small feet (tumblers are an exception). Colors are white, blue, and canary in opalescent glass, and amber, blue, and clear in crystal. Shapes known in opalescent glass are water sets, table sets, berry sets, (sometimes triangular in shape), celery vase, toothpick holder, finger bowls, and mugs.

Overlapping Leaves (Leaf Tiers)

While it has been reported as a Northwood product, this pattern has long been known by carnival glass collectors as a Fenton pattern called Leaf Tiers. In opalescent glass the colors are white, blue, and green, but amethyst is a strong possibility. Shapes are the rose bowl (shown), a bowl, and a plate, all footed and from the same mould.

Overlapping Leaves

Palisades (Lined Lattice)

Here is yet another pattern first credited to the Northwood Company but known to be a Dugan/Diamond product. Carnival glass collectors call this pattern Lined Lattice, where it can be found in stretched vases and even a light shade for a table lamp called the Princess Lamp. Colors in opalescent glass are white, blue, green, and canary. Vase and novelty bowls are from the same mould.

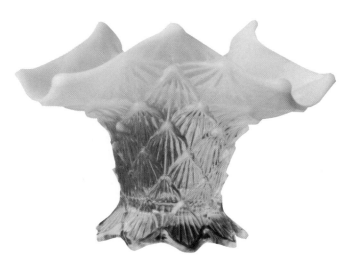

Palisades

Palm and Scroll

Palm Beach

Panelled Holly

Palm and Scroll

Credited to the Northwood Company in 1905, Palm and Scroll is actually a product of the Dugan Glass Company and was produced in opalescent glass beginning in 1906, in blue, green, and white. Shapes are various bowls on feet and a neat rose bowl from the same mould. The design is easily recognized; three palm leaves over the curled and ribbed feet and three very artistic feather scrolls between these designs.

Palm Beach

Made by the U.S. Glass Company, Palm Beach was originally their #15119 and can be found in a wide variety of shapes in both carnival glass and opalescent glass. In the latter, shapes known are water sets, table sets, berry sets, a jelly compote, and a large sauce dish or finger bowl. Colors are blue, white, and canary, with the latter having very strong coloring. Palm Beach dates from 1906, and was continued in production in other forms of glass treatment for several years.

Panelled Holly

Found in water sets, table sets, berry sets, novelty bowl shapes, and salt shakers, this pattern comes from the Northwood Glass Company and dates to 1904. Most pieces are considered rare and the only colors in opalescent glass are white and blue. The pattern was also made in limited amounts in carnival glass and crystal that is often decorated and in green decorated glass.

Peacocks

Peacocks (on the Fence)

Perhaps one of Northwood's best known patterns, especially in carnival glass, Peacocks on the Fence is found only on bowls or plates. Besides opalescent glass and carnival, a rare example of opaque or marbleized glass that was iridized is well known. The pattern dates from 1908 and in opalescent glass can be found in white, blue, and cobalt. (I suspect canary will eventually show up.) All these opalescent colors are quite scarce as small amounts must have been made.

Peacock Tail

While a casual glance may mistake this rare tumbler for the pressed Drapery, this Fenton tumbler is quite different. Note the octagon base and design that ends about ¾" below the lip. Just why the Fenton Company decided to make this one item in opalescent glass is a mystery since many shapes are known in carnival (but no tumbler!). I have seen a white opalescent example also and certainly green is a strong possibility.

Pearls and Scales

This pattern is credited to the Northwood Company, made in 1905 or 1906. It has been seen in a compote and a stemmed rose bowl from the same mould. Colors are white, blue, green, vaseline, and emerald. Sometimes, a cranberry edging is present, indicating this treatment wasn't exclusively Jefferson's.

Peacock Tail

Pearls and Scales

Pearl Flowers

Piasa Bird

Plain Jane

Pearl Flowers

Since this pattern is shown in Northwood ads as early as 1904, the maker of this very pretty pattern isn't hard to discern. It is found in bowls of all shapes, rose bowls and nut bowls, all footed and all from the same mould. Colors are white, blue, and green in opalescent glass. It has been reported in carnival glass but I have not seen it in my long years of carnival research and writing.

Piasa Bird

I must confess I am quite skeptical about the origin of this unusual pattern. It has many characteristics of English glass, but some trails lead toward American origin, namely Beaumont. It can be found in both white and blue opalescent glass and the shapes, all from a single mould, are rose bowls, a pulled vase shape, and a spittoon whimsey. All shapes are footed, and the feet remind me somewhat of those on the Inverted Fan and Feather pieces.

Plain Jane

I'm relatively sure this pattern came from the Dugan Company; this assumption is based on shape, color, and similarity to other Dugan pieces, chiefly nappies that are shaped the same. Over the years I've seen several Dugan Leaf Ray nappies with exactly the same shaping. Shown is the Plain Jane nappy in blue, but white and green were probably made. Production was most likely in the 1906 – 09 period.

Poinsettia

Found mainly on water sets but also known on syrups, bowls, and sugar shakers, this Northwood pattern is also known as Big Daisy. The pitcher shapes vary from a semi-cannonball type to three other tankard styles, and even a ring-necked one. Poinsettia dates from 1902, and can be found in white, cranberry, blue, green, and rarely canary. The tumblers are found in both pressed and blown examples and the bowl, which was made for use in a bride's basket, is most often found without a metal frame. Both the shaker and syrup are quite rare in any color and the tall tankard pitchers are very desirable.

Poinsettia

Poinsettia Lattice

Made by Northwood Glass, this very beautiful bowl pattern is known in carnival circles as Lattice and Poinsettia, where it is a somewhat rare and very prized pattern. In opalescent glass the colors are limited to white, blue, and vaseline. Production at the Northwood factory dates to 1907, and the latticework is exactly like that of a sister pattern called Cherry Lattice that followed a few years later in other types of glass.

Poinsettia Lattice

Popsicle Sticks

Credited to the Jefferson Glass Company, this is their #263 pattern. In design it is a simple series of wide unstippled rays that fan out from the center of the bowl shape. Colors are white, blue, and green opalescent glass, and it is found on large bowl shapes with a pedestal base. Shapes may be widely varied including ruffled edges, a banana bowl shape, and even a squared shape.

Popsicle Sticks

Pressed Coinspot

Prince Albert and Victoria

Prince William

Pressed Coinspot (#617)

First shown in a 1901 National Glass catalog, this compote (advertised as a card tray) was continued as a Dugan pattern, showing up in their ad for an Oriental assortment, labeled #617. In the vase shape, it later became known as Concave Columns and in carnival glass it is simply called Coinspot. Shapes from the same mould are tall vases, compotes, goblets, and a stemmed banana boat shape. Colors in opalescent glass are white, blue, green, and canary.

Prince Albert and Victoria

Most of the British production of opalescent glass dates from the late 1800s and was made by mostly three manufacturers: Sowerby & Company, Gateshead, England; George Davison & Company, Gateshead-on-Tyne; and Greener & Company of Sunderland, England. Shown is a very attractive creamer in a pattern called Prince Albert and Victoria. It is also known in an open sugar on a stem that looks like a small compote. Colors are blue and canary. This example was made by Davison.

Prince William

Shown is the breakfast set or the open sugar and creamer, made by Davison. Covered sugars were just not part of English glass production. This very attractive pattern can also be found in a beautiful oval plate and water set. Colors, as with most English opalescent glass production, are blue and canary.

Princess Diana

Here is another example of fine British opalescent production by Davison. Princess Diana is a pattern that can be found in many shapes, including a crimped plate, covered butter dish, open sugar, creamer, a water set, a matching tray for the water set, a biscuit set (jam jar with lid and matching plate), salad bowl, novelty bowls, and a compote with a fancy metal base. Colors are the usual blue and canary.

Pulled Loop

Well-known to the collectors of carnival glass, Pulled Loop is one of those very scarce Dugan patterns that was made in limited amounts in 1906, in opalescent glass. There are at least two sizes; I've seen 3" and 5" base diameters on these vases. The colors are white, green, and blue with many more green examples available than the other colors. There are six rows of "loop" columns and six rows of ribs that separate them.

Pump and Trough

Shown in a 1900 Pitkin and Brooks catalog, along with other Northwood Glass Company items, the very interesting Pump and Trough are listed as #566 and #567 respectively. Colors listed are white, blue, and canary. The design of these items typifies the trend toward naturalism in so many Northwood glass products (Grapevine Clusters, Ocean Shell, Leaf Chalice, and even the Dolphin compote), a trend that continued into their carnival production to some degree with the famous Town Pump. Of course, as with many good things, the Pump and Trough has been widely reproduced, so beware of pumps with flat tops!

Princess Diana

Pulled Loop

Pump and Trough

Queen's Petticoat

Q ueen's Petticoat

I believe this small bud vase is British and for that reason I've taken the liberty of naming it Queen's Petticoat for the ruffled base. In a way it reminds me of the William and Mary master salt as well as the three-handled whimsey shown elsewhere in this book. All have similar base scalloping. At any rate, it is a very attractive vase and was probably made in other colors including white and canary. I'd be happy to hear from anyone who can shed more light on this pattern.

Q uestion Marks

It is difficult to use only one name for this well-known Dugan pattern for it actually is not one but three patterns. The interior is called Question Marks, the exterior pattern is known as Georgia Belle, and the stem has a Dugan pattern called Puzzle! These compotes are mostly known in carnival glass, but here is the very rare example in a beautiful blue opalescent glass. I suspect it may have been made in white opalescent also, but no examples have been verified at this time.

R eflecting Diamonds

Let me say again, while they were both Dugan patterns, Reflecting Diamonds is not the same pattern as Compass. Having said that, please note Reflecting Diamonds appears in bowl shapes only and has been found as early as 1905, in Butler Brothers ads featuring Dugan/Diamond patterns. Like so many geometric patterns, this one has a series of diamonds filled with a file pattern bordered by fan shapes standing back-to-back between the diamonds. The base has the exact overlapping star design as that found on the Compass base.

Question Marks

Reflecting Diamonds

Regal

Reverse Swirl

Ribbed Opal Lattice

Regal

This pattern is certainly rightly named for it has a regal look. It was made by the Northwood Company in 1905, and some pieces are marked. Regal can be found in table sets, water sets, berry sets, salt shakers, and cruets in white, green, and blue opalescent glass as well as in crystal and emerald green glass with gilding. The pattern was also known as Blocked Midriff but the Regal name is most widely used.

Reverse Swirl

Made by the Buckeye Glass Company of Martin's Ferry, Ohio, and later in some degree by the Model Flint Glass Company of Albany, Indiana, this beautiful pattern dates from 1888. The lamp shown is from Buckeye and was made in two sizes. It is considered quite rare. Other shapes found are water sets, cruet, table sets, berry sets, salt shakers, syrups, sugar shaker, custard cup, mustard pot, toothpick holder, night lamps, a finger bowl, water bottles in two sizes, a caster set (four pieces in metal holder), and a very scarce tall salt shaker. Colors are white, blue, canary, and cranberry, and occasionally some items are satin finished.

Ribbed Opal Lattice

This is probably a Northwood Glass pattern, but may have been an earlier LaBelle Glass product. It is found in water sets, a cruet, salt shakers, syrup, table set, berry set, toothpick holder, sugar shakers in two sizes, and a celery vase. Colors are white, blue, and cranberry.

Ribbed Spiral

Richelieu

Ring Handled Basket

Ribbed Spiral

Made by the Model Flint Glass Company of Albany, Indiana, in 1902, this pattern can be found in a host of shapes including table sets, water sets, berry sets, plates, cups and saucers, toothpick holder, salt shaker, jelly compote, various bowls, and vases of all sizes. Colors are white, blue, and canary. The example shown is a beautiful plate.

Richelieu

Another of those very attractive British patterns, this one is from Davison and Company and dates to 1885. The RD number of this pattern is 96945 and items made are a jelly compote, creamer, divided dish, cracker jar, handled basket, various bowl shapes, and the neat handled nappy shown. Colors are white, blue, and canary.

Ring Handled Basket

As I've said before, I really think this is just another shape in Opal Open (or Beaded Panels as it is also known). At any rate, I will show it alone in the handled basket or handled center bowl shape. It is also found on salt shakers as well as the compote called Opal Open. Colors are blue and white, sometimes with a clam-broth effect. This coloring can be clearly seen in the ring just below the handle on the piece shown. This piece measures 7½" wide.

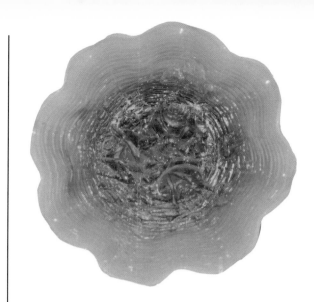

*R*ose Show
Known primarily as a carnival glass pattern, this very beautiful bowl can also be found in limited amounts in white and blue opalescent glass. Reputed to be a Northwood pattern, the bowl has a reverse pattern of Woven Wonder, a spin-off design of Frosted Leaf and Basketweave.

Rose Show

*R*ose Spatter
I am told by a reputable dealer and researcher that this very attractive pitcher with a ball shape came from either the Beaumont Glass Company or the Buckeye Company (both of Martins Ferry, Ohio). I haven't been able to verify either as the maker at this time. The coloring is much like the finish found on Northwood's Leaf Mold items called "tortoise shell spatter." At any rate, it's a super pitcher, and I believe it dates to the 1890s.

Rose Spatter

*R*oulette
Shown in a 1906 ad from a Lyon Brothers catalog, this Northwood pattern is very similar to the Diamond Point and Fleur-de-Lis pattern shown elsewhere. Many shapings were made from the bowl mould including a rose bowl, ruffled and flared bowls, and even a plate in white, blue, and green.

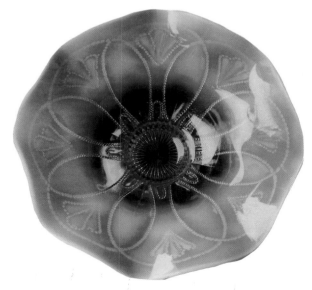

Roulette

Royal Scandal

Ruffled and Rings

Ruffles and Rings with Daisy Band

Royal Scandal

What a beautiful piece of glass work this British wall pocket vase is! It is very likely a product of Davison, minus the typical English RD number and measures some 6" in length. I've seen it in a beautiful blue opalescent as well as the canary one shown. The design seems to be a series of rope-like strips that cross over shell-type ribbing. At each side is a large petaled flower and the hanging band looks like thorny branches. The mould work and opalescence are simply outstanding. As far as I know, there is no known name for the pattern, so I've taken the liberty of providing a name; if I'm mistaken, I'll soon hear about it.

Ruffles and Rings

Originally another of the Jefferson Glass patterns that came into the Northwood production orbit, the opalescent version appears to have been made in 1906 and after. In carnival glass, the pattern has been found as an exterior one with such designs as Rosette, and even on a rare flint opalescent bowl with no interior pattern, marigold iridizing, and an added floral border edging. Colors in opalescent glass are white, blue, and green.

Ruffles and Rings with Daisy Band

Just why the Northwood Company decided to do this variant of the Ruffles and Rings pattern is a mystery, but here they've added a classy banding of daisies along the outer edge. Since both Jefferson and Northwood are credited with Ruffles and Rings, perhaps the regular is Jefferson's that was later made by Northwood who then added the band. At any rate, Northwood later made both versions in carnival glass and a very rare example of marigold with an opalescent daisy band exists. Opalescent colors are the usual white, blue, and green.

Ruffles and Rings with Daisy Band

S-Repeat

S-Repeat (National)

First advertised in a Butler Brothers ad of glass from the newly formed Dugan Glass Company, S-Repeat (or National as it was then called) seems to be a pattern designed while the plant was still operated by Northwood as a part of National Glass, but only released once Dugan had taken over. The ad dates to May, 1903. In opalescent glass, the colors made were white, blue, and green in limited amounts. Additional types of glass, including crystal, apple green, blue, and amethyst, were decorated and made in a wide range of shapes. In opalescent glass, shapes known are table sets, water sets, and berry sets. In addition, the goblet has now been found in blue opalescent (shown elsewhere in this book) formed into a compote shape with the Constellation pattern added to the interior.

Scheherezade

While the maker of this very pretty pattern has not been confirmed, I really believe we need look no further than the Dugan/Diamond Company. Found primarily in bowls, the opalescent colors are white, blue, and green. The design of file triangles, finecut triangles, and hobstars is a close cousin to Dugan's Reflecting Diamonds, but has more than enough difference to tell it from any other pattern. Scheherezade is a rather scarce pattern, but well worth looking for.

Scottish Moor

Made about 1890, this British pattern is a difficult one to find. It is known in water sets, a cruet, cracker jar, celery vase, and the ruffled vase shown. Colors are blue, white, cranberry (pitcher and tumblers only), rubina, and a pale amethyst. The glass has an airy look and while most items are blown, the ruffled vase and cracker jar are mould blown.

Scheherezade

Scottish Moor

Sea Spray

Scroll with Acanthus

Seaweed (Beaumont)

*S*croll with Acanthus

Credited to the Northwood Company, Scroll with Acanthus can be found in water sets, table sets, berry sets, a jelly compote, salt shaker, toothpick holder, and cruet. Colors are white, blue, and canary opalescent glass with some novelties in green opalescent, crystal, and purple slag, as well as decorated green and blue crystal. Production dates from 1903.

*S*ea Spray

Made by the Jefferson Glass Company in 1906 – 07, this was their #192 pattern. The only shape reported is the very attractive nappy and the colors are the usual white, green, and blue opalescent. The design is somewhat similar to the S-Repeat but has an interesting beading added below the "S" and sections of line filler above.

*S*eaweed (Beaumont)

Here is the Beaumont version of the old Hobbs, Brockunier Seaweed pattern. Beaumont Glass began making this pattern in 1895, in shapes that included oval shaped cruets; a finger bowl; round, tapered and square bitters bottles; and a water set with square top. Colors are white, blue, and cranberry but a canary opalescent rose bowl is known.

S*eaweed (Hobbs)*

Originally a Hobbs, Brockunier pattern, made in many shapes including water sets, salt shaker, syrup, table set, berry set, barber bottle, sugar shaker, pickle caster, cruet, and two sizes in oil lamps. Production dates to 1890, and colors known are white, blue, and cranberry. In addition, some items have a satin finish and the sugar shaker has turned up in purple slag glass, suggesting even the Northwood Company got into the act. (A Beaumont glass version is shown above.) Shown is the rare night lamp in pale cranberry.

Seaweed (Hobbs)

S*hell (Beaded Shell)*

While this Dugan pattern is known as Shell in opalescent glass, collectors of carnival and other types of glass recognize it as the Beaded Shell pattern. It was made in 1905, in a host of shapes including water sets, berry sets, cruet, toothpick holder, salt shaker, mug, and cruet set. Colors are white, green, blue, canary, electric blue, and apple green plus carnival colors.

Shell

S*hell and Wild Rose*

Called simply Wild Rose by carnival glass collectors this Northwood pattern dates from 1906. In opalescent glass it was made in white, blue, and green, but was later a part of their iridized production and is quite popular in carnival glass. The open edged inverted heart border is a wonder in glass work and must have been a mould maker's nightmare.

Shell and Wild Rose

77

Simple Simon

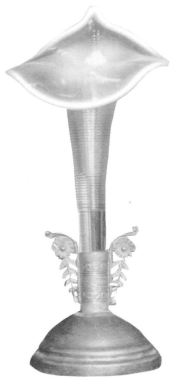

Single Lily Spool

Singing Birds

Simple Simon

Carnival glass collectors know this pattern as Graceful. It was a product of the Northwood Company dating from 1908 – 09. In carnival glass, it is made in most Northwood non-pastel colors, but in opalescent glass the colors are limited to green, white, and a scarce blue. While the design isn't too well planned, the compote's shape adds class, and the workmanship is quality.

Single Lily Spool

With the same threading around the base as the Spool compote credited to Northwood, this very attractive piece could be called a vase but the owner calls it an epergne and who am I to argue? The metal base has an Art Deco feel that adds so very much to the entire look and the opalescence is super. It probably came in white and perhaps other colors as well, but I can't verify this at this time.

Singing Birds

This famous Northwood pattern can be found in many types of glass including carnival, custard, and a clear glass decorated in blue, as well as the rare examples of the mug shape only in opalescent glass. First advertised in 1907 – 08 in blue or white opalescent, two rare examples of vaseline have been added to this limited production item. Highly collectible, these mugs bring top price and seldom trade owners.

Sir Lancelot

Advertised in a Butler Brothers ad in 1906, along with several well-known Northwood patterns, including Shell and Wild Rose, Diamond Point, and Hilltop Vines, Sir Lancelot is now recognized as a Northwood product. The shapes are novelty bowls with a dome base in white, blue, and green opalescent glass. The design, three fleur-de-lis and three starburst figures on a stippled background, is very interesting and quite attractive. The dome base is rayed.

Spanish Lace

Introduced by the Northwood Company to American collectors in 1899, this pattern has been known as Opaline Brocade, as well as its more popular name, Spanish Lace. Shapes made are water sets (three pitcher styles), table sets, cruet, salt shaker, wine decanter (very rare), night lamp, water bottle, perfume bottle, rose bowl, and a celery vase, as well as vases in several sizes. In addition several items are fitted with metal parts including a bride's basket and cracker jar. Colors are white, blue, and cranberry, with limited production of some shapes in green, and a few items in a canary that are likely of an English origin. A handled basket, a cruet, and a rose bowl have recently been made by Fenton in cranberry, but these are the only items that are not old. The pitcher shown is in the Ribbon Tie mould.

Spattered Coinspot

The shape of this very beautiful pitcher seems to be the same ball shape that Northwood used on the Daisy and Fern pitcher, but certainly it may well belong to another maker. I'm confident it is old, dating from the late 1800s, and as far as desirability is concerned it would have to be quite high. The coloring is simply beautiful with spatters of cranberry mixed with the flecks of white.

Sir Lancelot

Spanish Lace

Spattered Coinspot

Spokes and Wheels

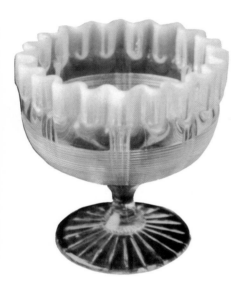

Spool of Threads

Squirrel and Acorn

Spokes and Wheels

Shown in a 1906 Butler Brothers ad along with several other Northwood Company patterns, Spokes and Wheels can be found in a variety of bowl shapes as well as plates that are tri-cornered or square. Colors are the usual white, blue, and green opalescent, but a rare aqua piece in a square plate exists.

Spool of Threads

Primarily a compote pattern, Spool of Threads is a Northwood pattern dating to 1905. It was advertised in 1902 in purple slag, and in opalescent glass it can be found in white, blue, canary, and perhaps green. I have heard of one item flattened out into a stemmed tray but haven't seen it.

Squirrel and Acorn

Here is one of the most appealing patterns in opalescent glass and in the whimsey section I show the vase. At this time, I do not know the maker of this pattern but can tell you it is quite rare, especially in blue and white. It was also made in a very scarce green. All shapes, a footed bowl, the compote, and the vase are from the same mould showing six panels with alternating designs of a frisky squirrel, acorn, and leaves. The base has a raised scale-like pattern. I'm sure the pattern dates to the 1904 – 10 era.

Stars and Stripes

While this pattern has been reproduced by the Fenton Company for the L.G. Wright Company, particularly in tumblers, a pitcher, and a small milk pitcher with reeded handle, the design originally came from Hobbs (1890) and later from Beaumont (1899). Original shapes were water sets, a barber bottle, cruet, finger bowl, and lamp shades. Colors were white, blue, and cranberry opalescent. The Wright reproduction cruets can be found with both ruffled and tri-cornered tops and both have reeded handles. Some of the repro items, especially the new water pitchers in blue, are very poorly done and the matching tumblers are thick and splotchy in coloring.

Stars and Stripes

Stork and Rushes

Found mostly in carnival glass in several shapes, this quite scarce mug and a tumbler are the only known shapes (thus far) in opalescent glass. Colors reported from Dugan Glass Company ads dating from 1909 are white and blue, but certainly green or vaseline may exist. There are two border bands on this pattern but as you can see, the opalescent pieces have the diamond file designed band at the top and bottom. The second banding, a series of dots, seems to appear only on carnival items.

Stork and Rushes

Stork and Swan

This very attractive syrup seems most likely to be of English origin. It is white with heavy opalescence from top to bottom. The handle is applied and the piece measures 5½" tall with a base width of 2¾". The metal lid is marked "Patd. Nov. 16th 1869." On one side is a very attractive Swan design featuring cattails and the floating swan, and on the reverse side, a stork (or crane) stands among cattails with a blooming tree on the opposite area. The rest of the piece is filled with vertical ribbing.

Stork and Swan

Stripe

Sunburst-on-Shield

Swag with Brackets

Stripe

Made by many glass companies including Northwood, Nickel-Plate, Jefferson, Buckeye, Beaumont, and even English production, Stripe (or Oval Stripe as it is also known) dates from 1886, and continued at one concern or another until 1905. Colors are white, blue, canary, cranberry, and even some rubina opalescent glass. Shapes include water sets with many shapes in pitchers, cruets, salt shakers of several shapes, syrups, finger bowls, sugar shakers, two caster sets, various oil lamps and miniature lamps, lamp shades, vases, celery vases, bowls, toothpick holder, barber bottle, wine decanter, several sizes in tumblers, and shot glasses. Reproductions are well known in the barber bottle, small 5" – 7" pitchers, and perhaps other shapes. I believe the example shown is Nickel-Plate glass.

Sunburst-on-Shield

While I will admit I much prefer the original Northwood name for this pattern (Diadem), I understand most collectors call it Sunburst-on-Shield. It dates to 1905, and in opalescent glass was made in table sets, berry sets, water sets, nappy, cruet, and the two-piece breakfast set shown. Colors are mostly blue and canary with some shapes in white known. The nappy and cruet are rare and the water set very scarce, as is a celery tray.

Swag with Brackets

Swag with Brackets is a product of the Jefferson Glass Company and dates to 1904. It can be found in white, blue, green, and canary opalescent glass, as well as crystal, amethyst, blue, and green, that are often decorated. Shapes are table sets, water sets, berry sets, toothpick holders, salt shakers, cruets, jelly compotes, and many novelties. Notice the cranberry fritt edging often found on Jefferson items.

Swastika

Shown on the Diamonds and Clubs mould, this Dugan/Diamond opalescent pattern can also be found on a ball-type pitcher mould, as well as on tumblers and a syrup. Colors are white, green, blue, and cranberry. The syrups can be found in both panelled and ball shapes. All pieces date from 1907 production and are quite scarce. It is a shame more shapes weren't developed in this pattern.

Swirl

Virtually every glass company who made opalescent glass had a Swirl design, and it is quite difficult to distinguish one maker's examples from the others except by shapes known to have been favored by some companies. It is for this reason I believe this pitcher and tumbler shown came from the Jefferson Glass Company, since it matches the shape of pitchers they made in both Swirling Maze and Lattice. Colors are blue, white, and cranberry, with green and canary strong possibilities. Notice that the handle is not reeded as on the Lattice pitcher in this shape. (The Swirling Maze also has no reeding.)

Swirl (Northwood Ball Shape)

Here's another look at one of the many Swirl patterns. This one is on Northwood's ball shape in the water set. This shape was also made by the Dugan Company and dates to (Hobb production) 1890. The Northwood version is sometimes called a variant. Colors are primarily white, blue, and cranberry, although rare examples of canary are known.

Swastika

Swirl

Swirl (Northwood Ball Shape)

Swirling Maze

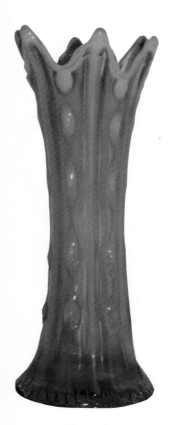

Target

Thread and Rib

Swirling Maze

While the ruffled salad bowls are known to have come from the Jefferson Glass Company (1905), there is some question about who made the various pitchers and tumblers in this pattern. (The pitchers have been found in three shapes.) Colors are white, blue, green, canary, and cranberry. I personally feel all pieces had the same maker and list the water sets as Jefferson also until proven wrong. I would be very surprised if additional shapes weren't made and eventually come to light.

Target

What a privilege it is to show this rare Dugan/Diamond vase, for like the Pulled Loop shown elsewhere, these were made in very limited amounts. I've only heard of the green so far, but surely a white opalescent one exists and we can dream of blue! Of course, this pattern is found primarily in carnival glass, usually in peach opalescent.

Thread and Rib

Harry Northwood must have been fascinated with epergnes. He designed the one shown here in 1906. He patented two additional designs, the well-known Wide Panel epergne in 1909 and a universal tube-receiving pedestal apparatus in 1916. The Thread and Rib epergne is shown in a 1906 Northwood catalog as #305 Flower Stand. It measures 18" tall and was available in white, blue, and green opalescent glass, although the example shown is vaseline opalescent and must have been an addition to the line. The base dish measures 12" and has threading below the metal and glass lily fittings. It sold in an assortment of nine for $7.50!

Threaded Optic

Threaded Optic

While I've named this pattern Threaded Optic, it could well be called "Inside Ribbing with Threading" as well. It may well be a spin-off pattern from the well-known Inside Ribbing pattern made by the Beaumont Glass Company of Martins Ferry, Ohio, but it has the look and coloring of a Dugan product. I've only seen the rose bowl in blue opalescent, but it certainly could have been made in other colors and shapes from the same mould such as bowls, plates, or vases. The ribbing or optic is all interior and the threading or horizontal rings are on the outside. The marie is plain and slightly raised. Also called Band and Rib.

Three Fruits

Dating from 1907, this Northwood pattern is mostly known in carnival glass production, but it was also made in limited amounts in opalescent glass in white and blue. The exterior pattern is called Thin Rib and the interior pattern of cherries, pears, and apples with leaves is an attractive one.

Three Fruits and Meander

In carnival glass this pattern is known as Three Fruits Medallion because of the leaf medallion in the interior's center. The meander pattern is on the exterior and shows through nicely with the pattern of fruits and leaves on the inside. This is a Northwood pattern and is found on both white and blue opalescent glass and many colors of carnival.

Three Fruits

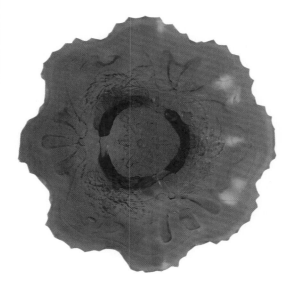

Three Fruits and Meander

Tines

Tiny Tears

Tokyo

Tines

Since I haven't been able to find another name for this beautiful vase (I suspect it may be British in origin), I named it Tines after the fork-like ridges that run vertically on the exterior from top to bottom. It also has a nice interior optic or ribbing. The opalescence is around the neck where the glass color is actually blue instead of the green found on the rest of the vase! This beauty stands 9½" tall and is very graceful indeed. The quality of the glass is very fine.

Tiny Tears

Very little information seems to be available for this vase although it appears to have the same coloring as so many vase patterns from either Northwood or Dugan/Diamond. The example shown stands 14" tall, has a rayed marie with 28 rays and an extended ridge above the base with fine ribbing on the inside, all around the base. I'm sure this was made in the usual opalescent colors and must have come from the 1903 – 10 era of production.

Tokyo

Made by the Jefferson Glass Company, Tokyo is a very distinctive pattern that can be found in table sets, water sets, berry sets, salt shakers, cruet, jelly compote, toothpick holder, vase, and a footed plate. Colors are white, blue, and green in opalescent glass and plain crystal, decorated blue and apple green glass. A few years ago Tokyo was reproduced in some shapes including the compote, so buy with caution.

*T*ree of Love

The maker of this very nice pattern, seen only in white opalescent glass so far, is a mystery, however, I strongly feel it is a British pattern. Shown are two of the shapes known, the compote and the plate. The interior design is one of leaves, stems, and flowers, but the leaves look like hearts! In the base is a series of nine diamonds circled by beading. The stem of the compote looks very unusual with a bolt- and nut-like configuration. I believe the pattern dates to the early 1900s.

*T*ree Stump

While this very interesting mug shape is usually called just Stump, the formal name is Tree Stump. The mould work is very good as is the coloring and the opalescence. Most collectors feel this item is from the Northwood Company and I agree it certainly has all the attributes of Harry Northwood's quality. In size it is shorter than most mugs and the very realistic tree branch handle and the knots on the bark add real interest. Colors are green, white, and blue opalescent and all are rather scarce.

*T*ree Trunk

This well-known Northwood vase is sometimes marked and was made in several sizes in carnival glass, including a huge example with an 8" base diameter called an elephant vase. In opalescent glass, I know of only the standard size (3¼" base) that can be stretched from 7" to 14" in height. Opalescent colors are white, green, and blue and date from 1907 – 08. Besides carnival glass and opalescent glass, Tree Trunk can be found in Northwood's Opal (milk glass), Ivory (custard glass), or a rare color called Sorbini, a blue marbled opaque glass with a marigold iridized spray coating.

Tree of Love

Tree Stump

Tree Trunk

Trout

Twigs

Twister

*T*rout

What a quality piece of glasswork this bowl is! I certainly wish I knew more about it; I suspect is may be European, possibly French. It is 8¼" in diameter, stands 3½" tall, and has a 4½" collar base. The design is very detailed with artistic fish around the sides and three Roman Key bars around the edge of the collar base. It may have been made in other colors and I dream of a blue one, but the white opalescent is the only one I've seen. Can anyone tell me more about it?

*T*wigs

First advertised in 1898 as a Northwood product in opalescent glass, the Twigs pattern was another of those patterns later produced by Dugan/Diamond once Northwood left the Indiana, PA, plant. In opalescent glass, Twigs is found in two sizes (the smaller 5" size and a slightly larger 6½" example) and is known in blue, white, green, and canary. In carnival glass, Dugan later made the same twig footed vase and a sister vase without twig feet called Beauty Bud Vase. These Dugan vases can be found in marigold, amethyst, peach opalescent, and I recently saw a strange tortoise-shell-over-marigold example that must have been an experimental item.

*T*wister

Found primarily in bowls in white, green, and blue opalescent, very scarce plates are also known. The maker has not been established, at least to my knowledge, but the base design of a radiating star is much like that found on the Carousel pattern which is known to be a Jefferson Glass product.

Universal Northwood Tumbler

When the Northwood Company produced Alaska and Klondyke (Fluted Scrolls or Jackson), the same tumbler mould was used for both patterns. By adding an enameled design (forget-me-nots for Alaska, daisies for Fluted Scrolls), the company not only saved money but produced similar but distinctive patterns. I am showing one of these tumblers without the enameling to show the design as it came from the mould. Naturally it came in all colors of each pattern and was made in opalescent glass, custard, crystal, and emerald green. In addition to the tumbler, a similar universal salt shaker was produced for these patterns.

Victorian Stripe with Flowers

While this is certainly pure art glass like so many items of the 1890s, I felt one piece of decorated glass with applied floral sprays might be in order to set a bit of perspective as to where the opalescent glass craze started before it progressed into the mostly pressed items we show elsewhere. This beautiful 10" vase is likely British and is tissue-paper thin, with stems of applied clear glass and flowers that have a cranberry beading. Notice the flaring base, much like many Northwood tankard pitchers that came later.

Vintage

This exterior pattern on 8" – 9" bowls with dome bases is yet another of those patterns first made by Jefferson in opalescent glass and later at the Northwood plant in Wheeling. The Northwood products in carnival glass usually compliment an interior pattern such as Rosettes or Three Fruits but the Vintage exteriors are all from the Jefferson moulds. Jefferson called this pattern #245 and colors are white, blue, and green with the white occasionally being decorated with a goofus painted treatment.

Universal Northwood Tumbler

Victorian Stripe with Flowers

Vintage

Vulcan

War of Roses

Waffle

Opalescent Glass, 1880 – 1930

Vulcan

When I first received the photo of this very attractive spooner, I was quite puzzled about the pattern. Only after a good deal of digging and some mental compromising did I come to the conclusion this is the Vulcan pattern, first made at National Glass in 1900, and then at Ohio Flint Glass of Lancaster, Ohio, in 1902. The crystal items known in this pattern are staggering and include table sets, toothpick holders, salts, 8" compote, celery vase, sauce, syrup, cruet, wine, olive dish, and a vase, but at this point we can only surmise the table set was made in opalescent glass. If anyone has additional information, I'd certainly like to know.

War of Roses

A pretty pattern from England's George Davison & Company, War of Roses can be found in either blue or canary opalescent glass (I suspect white was also made) in novelty bowls and the boat-shaped bowl on tiny feet that is shown. The pattern dates from 1885, and is quality in all ways. The design is not really a true rose and more closely resembles a stylized shell, with a row of beading along the bottom.

Waffle

I know very little about the origin of this attractive epergne except it originally came from Germany, carried by hand aboard a commercial airline a few years ago. It stands some 20" tall on an ornate metal base and the lily fits into a metal cup. The beautiful waffle design is olive green, shading to an attractive pink just before the opalescent edging starts. The glass is very fine and thin and is mould blown.

Waterlily and Cattails

Waterlily and Cattails

While both the Fenton Art Glass Company and the Northwood Company had examples of this pattern in other types of glass, chiefly carnival glass, only the Fenton Company made the opalescent pieces. Shapes known are a table set, water set, berry set, tri-cornered bon-bon, square bon-bon, handled relish, bowl novelties, plates, and a breakfast set consisting of an individual creamer and sugar. Colors are white, green, blue, and amethyst, and carnival glass colors.

Wheel and Block

Shown as early as 1905 in ads with other Dugan Glass patterns, Wheel and Block has been seen in deep bowls, a vase whimsey and a square plate, all from the same mould. Colors are blue, green, and white with the latter sometimes having a goofus treatment as on the square plate shown.

Wheel and Block

Wide Panel

Here is the second Northwood epergne design, called Wide Panel or Colonial by some collectors. It is well known in carnival glass and is equally respected in opalescent colors of green, white, or blue. Notice that the four lily receiving tubes have been moulded into the glass and the whole design sweeps in a wide paneling from lily to the base. It is less formal than the first epergne design, Thread and Rib, and has no metal in the fittings at all! The fall Butler Brothers catalog of 1909 lists this in opalescent colors at $1.25 each and the 1913 April catalog from the same concern has the carnival glass at $1.50 a piece! How times have changed.

Wide Panel

Wild Daffodils

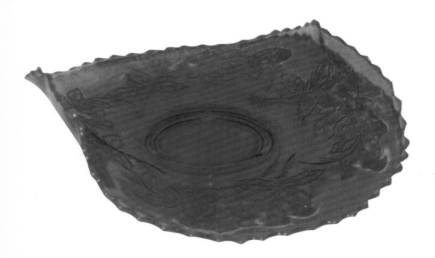

Wild Rose

William and Mary

Wild Daffodils

When I first saw this mug pattern, I thought the design was the same as the Wild Rose banana bowl shown elsewhere, but on closer examination, it is obvious the floral design in different. The shape of the mug is like Fenton's Orange Tree mug and I feel it is a Fenton pattern. Colors known are amethyst opalescent, white opalescent with gold trim, and the very strange example shown which looks like a thin custard with the same opalescence and gilding. I believe production of this mug dates from the 1909 – 11 era.

Wild Rose (Fenton's)

While I have no proof this interesting pattern is from the Fenton Art Glass Company, I feel safe enough to say I believe it is. First of all, the coloring is a deeper blue that matched known Fenton opalescent production items like Waterlily and Cattails, Honeycomb and Clover, Beaded Stars, and the Hobnail atomizer made for DeVilbiss. In size, the Wild Rose bowl is generous (the banana bowl measures 10½" in length) and the design is simply a raised line drawing just as that found on the Wild Daffodils mug shown above. I haven't tracked any other colors but it was probably made in white opalescent and perhaps green or amethyst.

William and Mary

William and Mary is a Davison Glass product, made in 1903, and found in the usual English opalescent colors of vaseline (canary) and blue. Shapes known are table sets (creamers and open sugars), compotes, a master salt, stemmed cake plate (made from the compote shape), flat plates, and novelty items. The distinctive design elements are the hearts on a line separated by areas of diamond filing.

Wilted Flowers

While this pattern is listed as from an unknown maker until now, I strongly suspect it came from the Jefferson Glass Company. I base this on the three-one-three crimp of the edges, so typical of many Jefferson patterns as well as the sunburst design of the base that is like Twister, suspected to be from Jefferson, and Carousel, a known Jefferson pattern. Colors are the usual white, blue, and green.

Windflower

Known to be a Dugan Glass Company product that is better known in carnival glass than in opalescent, where it is considered rather rare. First advertised in 1907, the opalescent colors are known in white and blue and in a 1914 Butler Brothers ad they can be seen along with equally rare opalescent patterns like the Mary Ann vase, the Constellation compote (pulled from the S-Repeat or National goblet shape with an added interior pattern), a Fishscales and Beads bowl, and Stork and Rushes mug and tumbler. A green opalescent Windflower bowl would be a great rarity, but I have no knowledge that one even exists.

Windows (Plain)

Originally a Hobbs, Brockunier pattern, it was later produced by Beaumont Glass and dates to 1889. Shapes known are water sets, finger bowls, bitters bottles, a crimped bowl, oil lamps in several shapes, and two sizes of miniature lamps. Colors known are white, blue, and cranberry. The beautiful pitcher shown has the square top and is a sight to behold.

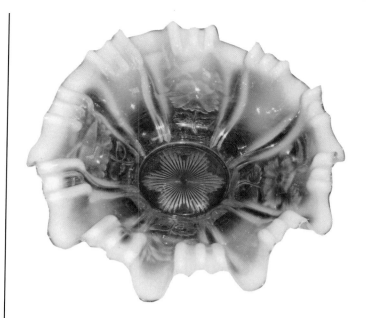

Wilted Flowers

Windflower

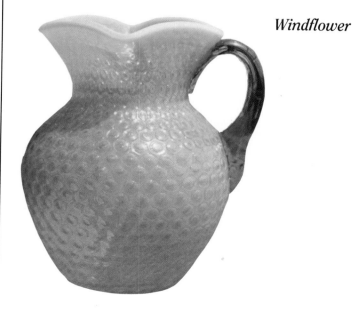

Windows

Winter Cabbage

Wishbone and Drapery

Woven Wonder

Winter Cabbage

This Dugan pattern very closely resembles another pattern called Cabbage Leaf, also made at Dugan. Both patterns date from 1906, and the difference is the number of leaves, with Winter Cabbage having only three and Cabbage Leaves having overlapping leaves. Winter Cabbage is known in bowls that rest on three vine-like feet that bend back and join the drooping marie of the bowl. Colors are white, green, and blue in opalescent glass.

Wishbone and Drapery

A Jefferson Glass product from 1903, Wishbone and Drapery is found on bowls and plates in white, green, and blue opalescent. While the design is a pleasant one, it didn't take much imagination and could not be called exciting. However, the coloring is nice, especially on the blue pieces.

Woven Wonder

Made by the Northwood Company, Woven Wonder is actually the same pattern as the exterior of the Rose Show bowl and even the same as Frosted Leaf and Basketweave without the leaf. Perhaps the latter's sugar base was flared for these exterior patterns but I can't prove it. At any rate, Woven Wonder can be found in novelty bowls like the tricornered one shown, as well as rose bowls, and I suspect even a vase could be in the realm of possibility. Colors reported are white and blue, but green and canary may well have been made.

Wreath and Shell

Wreath and Shell

Made in a wide variety of colors and types of glass, Wreath and Shell can be found in white, blue, and vaseline opalescent glass, as well as crystal, decorated crystal, and gilded. The pattern was made by the Model Flint Glass Company of Albany, Indiana, around 1900, and can be found in water sets, table sets, berry sets, celery vase, toothpick holder, rose bowl, lady's spittoon, cracker jar, salt dip, and novelties including bowls.

Wreathed Cherry

While some of these opalescent items in this well-known Dugan/Diamond Glass Company pattern are suspected to be reproductions, this very pretty creamer looks old to me. The glass quality is identical to other Dugan items of the 1909 period and the opalescence is outstanding. There is some wear on the base and the glass weight is more like old. At any rate, you should buy with caution. Shapes reported are table set pieces, but in carnival glass water sets, table sets, oval berry sets, and a very questionable toothpick holder are known. *Never buy this toothpick holder in opalescent glass, for all are new!*

Wreathed Cherry

Zipper and Loops

This large vase was a Jefferson Glass Company product, dating from 1908. It can be found in the usual opalescent glass colors of green, white, and blue. While attractive, it certainly isn't a showstopper, but it does fit very nicely in a collection of vases and is of a useable size being some 11½" tall.

Zipper and Loops

Part II: *Whimsey Pieces*

Webster's Dictionary defines a whimsey as an odd fancy and that definition certainly fits the glass items in this section.

Generally speaking, the glassmakers were very skilled artisans and liked nothing better than to show off these skills. Often, when they grew bored or tired of the same shapes being turned out, they produced one of these odd fancies that was not a part of regular production but could nevertheless be sold as either a novelty or sometimes given to a friend or loved one as a special gift. Many whimsies were made to be slipped out of the factory by the glassmaker at the end of the day, to be taken home and presented to a wife or family member.

For these reasons, whimsies have become a very loved part of glass collecting and it is a pleasure to show a few examples here so that the collector of today may understand just what whimsies are and how attractive they may be.

And perhaps I should also say that some whimsies were so popular they did go into limited production from pattern to following pattern. Such examples of lady's spittoons as I show here became very popular and were produced over the years on many types of glass, especially in the years of carnival glass production, until they were no longer considered whimsies at all!

Many whimsies, however, are a bit grotesque in their shaping and seem strange indeed to us today. Just remember, every one of these odd fancies was the product of a master craftsman in the days when glassmaking was an art. Enjoy them!

Argonaut Shell Tray

*A*rgonaut Shell (Nautilus) Tray

This whimsey item was originally the sugar base in the table set before it was stretched and turned into this very attractive whimsey card tray. As you can see, the color is vaseline but it can be found in white and blue as well. This piece is one of those whimsies that were apparently quite popular for they were made in some number.

*C*ashews Rose Bowl

Apparently the Northwood Company permitted artistic license in workers, for many whimsey shapes came from this company. Here is the pretty Cashews pattern, normally found on bowls or plates, but pulled up and ruffled into a stunning rose bowl. When I first saw this piece I fell in love with it and would sure love to own a blue one!

*D*aisy and Plume

What makes this footed bowl a whimsey is not only the depth of the bowl but the very odd way the top is ruffled into square shapes. I can't recall another pattern with this exact same crimping, either from Northwood or Dugan.

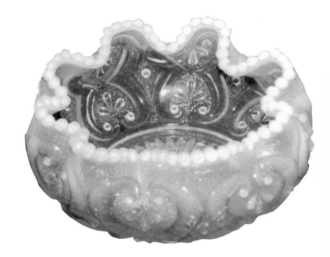

Cashews Rose Bowl

Daisy and Plume

Fan Card Tray

Feathers Bowl

*F*an Card Tray

A bit flatter than the Argonaut Shell card tray whimsey shown earlier, this piece shows the Dugan/Diamond Glass workers were just as skilled. This piece was made from the spooner in the table set. Two of the edges have been extended to elongate the piece and add interest. Oddly enough, this pattern was also whimsied into a gravy boat with handle that is often found in carnival glass.

*F*eathers Bowl

Here is a real rarity! Pulled from the well-known Northwood vase pattern, this is the *only* example of the whimsey bowl shape I've ever seen or heard about. It certainly is an outstanding item. Surely more were made but where are they? The vase can be found in blue and green also, so keep your eyes open. This piece has a base diameter of 3⅝", is 2½" high, with a bowl diameter of 8½".

*F*lora Banana Bowl

Flora is a Beaumont Glass pattern and the whimsey shown was made from the butter dish base. The top has been pulled to make it oval and then heavily ruffled giving it a very pretty look. I've heard there is one of these with an applied handle spanning the center but haven't seen it. The same shape with a handle does appear in many later items, especially from the Dugan/Diamond Company in carnival glass.

Flora Banana Bowl

*Inverted Fan and Feather
Spittoon*

Inverted Fan and Feather Spittoon

Here is one of the very attractive spittoon whimsey pieces, again from Northwood, pulled from the spooner shape. In carnival glass, these pieces are called lady's spittoons, for rumor has it that women actually were the users! I can't verify this, but my great-grandmother did smoke a clay pipe so maybe they were tobacco chewers, too.

Inverted Fan and Feather Card Tray

I fell in love with this cutie the first time I saw it and am not ashamed to say so. It was whimsied from the jelly compote and is a real find. I've seen blue and vaseline but white surely is known.

Inverted Fan and Feather Rose Bowl

Also from the spooner shape, this whimsey item was so popular it was actually produced in greater amounts and eventually even advertised by the Northwood Company. It was long felt by some collectors to be a new item but that proved to be untrue since this whimsey piece was advertised in a 1901 National ad after Northwood's admission into the combine.

Inverted Fan and Feather Card Tray

*Inverted Fan and Feather
Rose Bowl*

*Inverted Fan and
Feather Vase*

Jewels and Drapery Bowl

Keyhole Bowl

*I**nverted Fan and Feather Vase*

Shown in a 1908 Butler Brothers ad of Dugan/Diamond items, this very scarce vase was a carryover at the factory and was made in limited amounts in blue, green, and white opalescent glass. It is the first I've been privileged to see.

*J**ewels and Drapery Bowl*

Here is the whimsey bowl shape that was flattened from the vase shape shown elsewhere. While the vase is a difficult item to find, the whimsey is just plain rare!

*K**eyhole Bowl*

Here is an example of a whimsey that is like the original shape. The only thing that qualifies this piece as a whimsey is the tri-cornered shape of the top and the dipping of one side of the triangle like a jack-in-the-pulpit shape. This configuration was quite popular and all companies made some bowls in similar shapes, especially in the carnival glass era. Keyhole is a Dugan/Diamond item and was made in goofus, carnival, and opalescent glass.

Leaf and Beads Bowl

Leaf and Beads Bowl

Generally found in a rose bowl or candy bowl shape, this piece has been stretched into a rough triangle and then had the three corners reshaped to give it a very odd look. One corner has been pulled down, the other two are almost level and the back area opposite the dropped corner is raised!

Leaf and Beads (Flame)

Shaped much like the other whimsey shown in this pattern, this example has the flames on the edging pulled to very exaggerated points, making this an attractive and unusual piece.

Many Loops Tri-Cornered Bowl

The tri-cornered effect on this Jefferson bowl is quite easy to see and typifies the crimping that gives this very nice shaping. Please remember the tri-cornered bowls generally sell for about 20 percent more than round ones, so its a point to look for.

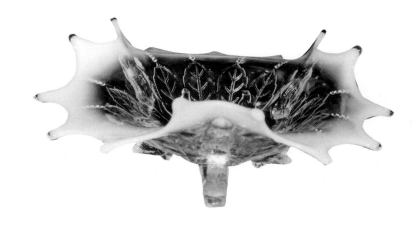

Leaf and Beads (Flame)

Many Loops Tri-Cornered Bowl

Ocean Shell

Piasa Bird Spittoon

Piasa Bird Vase

O cean Shell

Not as obvious as some whimsey pieces, this Ocean Shell relies on the one edge being pulled out to form a tail-like section while the opposite side has been scooped into a small spout. It is almost as if the glassmaker wanted to form a gravy boat without the handle!

P iasa Bird Spittoon

Probably no other pattern in opalescent glass can be found in more whimsey shapes than this one. This one is the spittoon shape and while it became an in-line item, it is nevertheless a whimsey shape as are all spittoons. All Piasa Bird whimsey pieces were shaped from the bowl shape.

P iasa Bird Vase

Much like the regular vase in this pattern, this whimsey has one top flame pulled into a grotesque spike and it is for this reason it has to be called a whimsey. Just what the glassmaker had in mind is hard to imagine. Surely he didn't just have a bad day, for several of these vase whimsey pieces are known.

Piasa Bird Rose Bowl

*P*iasa Bird Rose Bowl

Here is the third whimsey in this pattern and it really shows the design as well as any piece I've seen. For some reason, blue seems to the be the color most found in these pieces and I've seen more rose bowls than spittoons. Oddly, some collectors know this pattern by other names (Old Man of the Sea or Demonic) but Piasa seems to be the name most used.

*R*oulette Square Plate

Just as tri-cornered bowls are very collectible, so are squared plates and bowls. Here, the standard Roulette bowl has been first flattened to a plate and then the four opposing corners pulled to a square, making a very pleasing design.

*S*quirrel and Acorn Vase

If you will compare this with the standard compote in this pattern shown earlier you will see just how much of a whimsey this piece has become, especially with the three flattened flames that are almost comical. But despite this odd shaping, this piece is quite attractive and would add much to any collection, especially since the pattern is so very rare.

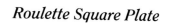

Roulette Square Plate

*Squirrel and Acorn
Vase*

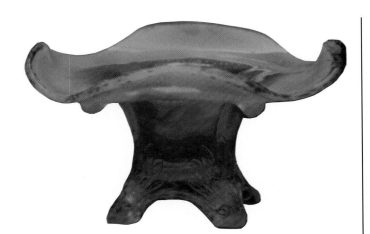

Swag with Brackets Sugar Base

Twigs Vase

Wreath and Shell Spittoon

Swag with Brackets Sugar Base

Just why Jefferson made these whimsey pieces from the sugar base is a mystery to me! And then to top them with the cranberry fritt edging seems to be a bit much; nevertheless, I've seen these in all the opalescent colors Jefferson made and all had the cranberry decoration (a few even had gilding on the legs). I suppose they could be used as nut or mint dishes!

Twigs Vase

This Dugan vase is one of the prettiest whimsies made and for this reason was produced in some amounts although not nearly so many as to be production shaping for more than a few months. As you can see, the top has been opened and pulled into four wing-like ruffles that really give life and character to this vase and make it much more attractive than the regular shapings shown elsewhere in this book.

Wreath and Shell Spittoon

Made by the Model Flint Glass Company of Albany, Indiana, this pattern had several whimsey versions, all from the table set spooner and I am showing three of these. Here is the spittoon and there seems to be several examples of this shape in blue, white, and canary. All are quite collectible and sought after by advanced buyers.

Wreath and Shell Rose Bowl

Wreath and Shell Rose Bowl

Just like the spittoon whimsey previously shown, this piece came from the spooner shape and had the lips turned in to make a rose bowl. I think this shape is much prettier than the spittoon whimsey, but fewer of these seem to be around. Maybe they just didn't survive as well. At any rate, they are very collectible and highly prized.

Wreath and Shell Nut Bowl

Here is the third whimsey in this pattern and it is the hardest to find and, I feel, the prettiest of all. As you can see, the sides have just the slightest flare at the top and are almost straight, giving it the shape known to collectors as a nut bowl.

Wreath and Shell Nut Bowl

Part III: *Opalescent Glass After 1930*

Wherever I've gone to photograph items for this book, I've found examples of glass made after the time frame generally accepted as old opalescent glass. Some of this newer glass is very attractive in its own right and some is an obvious attempt to copy old patterns.

For the sake of identification I've decided to show a sampling of these items so that the collector will be aware of them but I purposely *do not price these new items* since I catalog *only old glass*.

Actually an entire book could be filled with new items and many more are being produced every year; with the examples here we are only breaking the surface. When collecting, be alert, handle as much glass and you can, study it (both old and new). You will soon be able to tell a difference and in most cases will not find yourself paying huge prices for new glass or reproductions.

Remember, the majority of the patterns (approximately 90 percent) *have not been reproduced!* Of course, I do not have to tell you that patterns like Hobnail, Coinspot, Swirl, and Stripe have many copies and should only be purchased as old once you are comfortable with your knowledge. Buy only from a reputable dealer who will stand behind the sale if you do suspect your purchase to be questionable.

Beyond that, all I can say is "Happy Hunting!"

Hobnail Atomizer

A tomizers

In the late 1920s and early 1930s the Fenton Company made beautiful glass atomizers for the DeVilbiss Company, who were marketers and producers of the metal atomizer parts. Since the DeVilbiss products have become quite collectible, these beautifully made glass ones are now sought by many collectors. Shown are three examples: Hobnail (1928), Cosmos FLower (1932), and Petticoats (1933).

F enton Daisy and Fern

This very attractive pitcher is shown in the 1983 L.G. Wright catalogs and was produced by Fenton for them. As you can see, the handle is reeded, a warning sign. Colors are cranberry, cobalt blue, and this beautiful vaseline. Now as far as buying such a nice piece, there certainly is a place for such quality in collecting as long as you know it is new and as long as you pay new prices for it.

Cosmos Flower Atomizer

Petticoats Atomizer

Fenton Daisy and Fern

Duncan and Miller Ashtray

Duncan and Miller Vase

Duncan and Miller

This well-known firm was organized in 1874, and over the years has made many types of glass. It is their opalescent items, made in the 1920s and 1930s that most impress collectors today. For this reason I'm showing two examples of their work. First, an ashtray in vaseline opalescent glass from a line known as Sanibel. It has a very modern look, came in many colors, and certainly would not be confused with old glass. Next is a pale blue opalescent vase called "Cogs et Plume." Its artistic quality is obvious and compares with items from Lalique glass.

Fenton Coindot Basket

First made about 1947, this basket shape has a lot of quality, as do nearly all Fenton products, but the giveaway as to age is two-fold. First is the shape, not found in old opalescent American glass and most prominent, the sectioned handled that so looks like bamboo. Remember, unless you are confident about age, always avoid reeded or sectioned handles!

Fenton Coindot Basket

Fenton Hobnail

Fenton Hobnail

While this Fenton pattern has been in production for more than 50 years in opalescent treatments, it remains one of their all-time sales leaders and the colors are as endless as the shapes made. Since 1970 they have marked their product with a permanent mark (earlier examples had paper stickers). Colors are blue, green, lime, topaz, cranberry, french opalescent, some in several shadings. Shapes include pitchers, tumblers, cruets, baskets, epergnes, candlesticks, slippers, colognes, vases in several shapes, and a vanity set.

Fenton's Hobnail Lamps

Shown are two very different lamps with blue opalescent hobnail founts that were made by the Fenton Glass Company in the early 1930s. These founts were supplied to several lamp makers who then turned out these very attractive lamps. Colors reported are blue, white, and cranberry.

Fenton's Hobnail Lamps

Fenton Swirl Bowl

Fenton Spanish Lace

Fenton Swirl Vase

Fenton Spanish Lace

This very pretty Fenton reproduction is so very well done, it compares favorably with old pieces, but aside from being marked, this piece has a reeded handle that has to be a warning! Just remember, the Fenton Company has made many patterns and pieces over the years in opalescent glass and most have been well cataloged in three Fenton books, so there is little reason to mistake these pieces. Add to that the fact that Fenton began marking all their glass in 1970, and the task becomes simple.

Fenton Swirl Bowl

Shown is a very attractive Swirl bowl made by the Fenton Glass Company in 1939. It sits atop one of their standards that were sold as both bowl stands and a base for the hurricane shades made at the time. These bases can by found in royal blue and milk glass.

Fenton Swirl Vase

The Fenton Company started making this vase in the 1930s, and it has been popular over the years. The company called this vase pattern Spiral. Other shapes are known, such as candlesticks, a console bowl, a 10½" triangle vase, and a large hat vase. The vase shown is 8" tall. Colors are varied including French opalescent, blue, green, cranberry, and possibly others. Some pieces have a contrasting cased edge.

Floral Eyelet

*F*loral Eyelet (Daisy Eye Dot)

Also made for the L.G. Wright Company by Fenton, this very nice copy is called Daisy Eye Dot in their advertising in 1982. The original pattern was the very rare Floral Eyelet, of course. Again the giveaways are the reeded handle and the shape of the pitcher (old Floral Eyelet pitchers are *not* cannonball shaped). However, there again is a new item well worth owning if you do not buy it as old and pay a new price for it.

*F*ostoria Heirloom

Here are three shapes that were all grouped in Fostoria's Heirloom line, made between 1959 and 1970. The bowl was listed as #2183, the star-shaped plate as #2570, and the rolled novelty bowl that I called Rolled Rib as #2727. This latter piece had several shapes including a deep bowl and the other two items were also available in more shapes. I've seen these items in green, white, cranberry (light), and two shades of blue, the one shown and a very light airy one. The quality of all these items is outstanding and should be collected with the best of glass items dating to the 1960s and 1970s.

Fostoria Heirloom

Hand Vase

Hand Vase

Despite being a newer item, made by Fenton in 1942 as their #38, I find this 4" cutie very attractive. It has the quality Fenton is known for and fairly good opalescence.

Hobnail (Czechoslovakian)

Made in the 1950s, these two pieces, a cranberry puff box with cover and a vaseline tumbler, are very pretty examples of the world famous Hobnail pattern, this time made in Czechoslovakia. Note that the hobs go all the way over the bottom of these pieces. I've seen several items including small dishes, a small vase, and perfume bottles that match the puff box. Colors I know about are cranberry, vaseline, a very dark blue, and a dark green.

Hobnail Puff Box

Hobnail Tumbler

Hobnail Variant

*H*obnail Variant

I've called this Hobnail pattern a variant because of the odd seam-like sections that are on opposite sides of the piece. I've named this a "zipper mould" because it looks just like a zipper's fittings to me. It was made in the late 1940s and early 1950s in several shapes. Quality-wise, it isn't top-notch.

*L*ace Edged Buttons

This Imperial pattern dates from 1937, and was still being made in 1942. I've seen more than one shape but all had the open-edged treatment. Colors are blue, green, or white, but there may well be others. While attractive, the value isn't much more than it was when these items were made.

Lace Edged Buttons

*L*ace Edged Diamonds

Like its close companion, Lace Edged Buttons, this is another Imperial pattern made in the late 1930s and early 1940s. As you can see, this pattern has handles. It is a very nice design, made in white, green, and blue, but again, the value is small and only slightly more than when manufactured.

Lace Edged Diamonds

Needlepoint

Open-Edge Basketweave

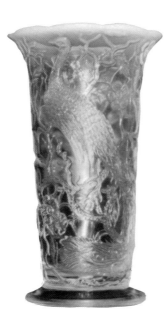

Peacock Garden Vase

Needlepoint

This is a Fostoria pattern and is signed on the bottom in script. These tumblers were made in three sizes and at least three colors including green (shown), blue, and orange. They first appear in Fostoria ads in 1951, and have no other shapes listed.

Open-Edge Basketweave

While Fenton made this very pattern in old opalescent glass in 1911 – 13, it wasn't made in this royal blue color until 1932, so we can be sure this is a newer piece. Old colors are blue (regular), green, and white, as well as a pastel vaseline.

Peacock Garden Vase

This very beautiful 10" vase in French opalescent glass was a product of the Fenton Company (their #791) and was made in 4", 6", 8", and 10" sizes in 1934. The moulds came from the old Northwood Company, it is believed, where a carnival version was made. Since the early 1930s, Fenton has made this vase (in the 8" size mostly) in over two dozen treatments including a topaz opalescent example in 1988. The 10" example shown is considered quite rare and is very collectible.

Plymouth

In 1935 Fenton made a large line of this pattern, all very useful items including plates, wines, highballs, old fashioned glasses, a rare mug, and this pilsner shown. These were all done in their French opalescent glass and have quality all the way. Additional shapes were added including a cocktail glass and a goblet.

Swan Bowl

Apparently this bowl and its companion pieces (smaller bowls and candlesticks) were first made at the Dugan/Diamond plant in 1926 – 27, and later at the Fenton Art Glass factory in 1934 – 39. The Dugan/Diamond version is known in pink, green, and black glass and the Fenton pieces are advertised in opalescent colors so it appears the master bowl shown is a Fenton item despite its color matching so many of Dugan's opalescent items in blue. At any rate, these blue pieces are considered rare as are the green opalescent items. Other treatments at the Fenton factory are satinized crystal (1939), amber (1938), amethyst (same year), and the large bowl is currently being made in a pretty misty green.

Tokyo

If you look closely at the compote shown you can see the color is light, the opalescence thin. The original pattern was made by Jefferson glass in 1905, but this piece when held and examined is obviously not of that quality. I do not know of other shapes having been reproduced but it is possible.

Plymouth

Swan Bowl

Tokyo

Price Guide

This price guide has been expanded to include in a complete, up-to-date manner, both American and English opalescent glass production from 1890 to 1930. This is a natural time frame for such glass and sets a distinctive break between antique glassware and contemporary production. Designed to supply prices for virtually all shapes and colors catalogued in this 40 year period, I know of no other reference that can duplicate this work. Prices followed by an asterisk (*) are speculative. The same mark (*) after a pattern name indicates this pattern has been reproduced in some shape(s). In a few instances, prices have been averaged where several varieties of a shape exist, but I have made a concerted effort to list prices as completely as possible.

Values were determined and tabulated from dealer's lists, shop taggings, antique guide listings, and personal speculation. Auction prices played only a minor role due to their often inflated bidding value. All items are priced as *mint* in condition and without flaw or color poorness, as well as being complete (American sugars have lids, British sugars are open compote shapes). *Please remember this is only a guide and prices herein are not set in stone. As with all guides it is meant to advise rather than set prices.*

Most pattern names conform to those used by William Heacock except where another name is more commonly accepted. In such cases I've included both names for reference.

I welcome comments from all collectors, but do ask that anyone who wants a reply, please include a self-addressed, stamped envelope with your correspondence. I especially encourage those letters that include information I have not had for this book; for this is how I learn and how my books improve with each edition.

	Blue	Green	White	Vaseline/Canary	Cranberry	Other	
Abalone							
Bowl	35.00		26.00	39.00			
Acorn Burrs (& Bark)							
Bowl, master	150.00		110.00				
Bowl, sauce	55.00		40.00				
Adonis Pineapple							
Claret bottle	365.00					395.00	Amber
Alaska							
Pitcher	395.00		350.00	375.00		450.00	Emerald
Tumbler	75.00		60.00	75.00		85.00	Emerald
Butter	390.00		295.00	400.00		290.00	Emerald
Sugar w/lid	170.00		140.00	165.00		165.00	Emerald
Creamer	90.00		70.00	85.00		80.00	Emerald
Spooner	90.00		70.00	85.00		80.00	Emerald
Bowl, Master	175.00		140.00	175.00		165.00	Emerald
Bowl, Sauce	65.00		30.00	60.00		60.00	Emerald
Cruet	300.00		260.00	290.00		285.00	Emerald
Tray	200.00		140.00	190.00		175.00	Emerald
Banana Boat	275.00		255.00	275.00		270.00	Emerald
Shakers, pair	150.00		75.00	140.00		95.00	Emerald
Bride's Basket	295.00		150.00				
Arabian Nights							
Pitcher	400.00		300.00	400.00	950.00		
Tumbler	75.00		50.00	70.00	120.00		
Syrup	250.00		195.00	275.00			
Argonaut Shell* (Nautilus)							
Pitcher	495.00		365.00				
Tumbler	120.00		95.00	100.00			
Butter	310.00		260.00				
Sugar	250.00		210.00				
Creamer	200.00		160.00				
Spooner	200.00		145.00				
Bowl, Master	150.00		120.00				
Bowl, Sauce	65.00		50.00				
Cruet	500.00		350.00				
Shakers, pair	100.00		75.00	85.00			
Jelly Compote	100.00		70.00	80.00			
Novety Bowls	65.00		45.00	95.00			

Add 15% for Script signed pieces

	Blue	Green	White	Vaseline/Canary	Cranberry	Other	
Ascot							
Bowl	60.00						
Creamer	85.00			90.00			

	Blue	Green	White	Vaseline/ Canary	Cranberry	Other
Astro						
Bowl	55.00	50.00	40.00	50.00		
Aurora Borealis						
Novelty Vase	65.00	80.00	50.00			
Autumn Leaves						
Bowl	60.00		45.00			
Banana Bowl	70.00		50.00			
Baby Coinspot*						
Syrup			135.00			
Vase		95.00		85.00		
Band and Rib (Threaded Optic)						
Rose Bowl	55.00		40.00			
Barbells						
Bowl	40.00	50.00	30.00	45.00		
Basketweave* (Open Edge)						
Console Set, 3 pcs.	240.00	260.00	190.00	250.00		
Nappy	50.00	40.00	37.00	45.00		
Bowl	45.00	40.00	35.00	40.00		
Plate	90.00	100.00	65.00	125.00		
Beaded Cable						
Bowl, Footed	50.00	40.00	30.00	46.00		
Rose Bowl, Footed	65.00	57.00	45.00	60.00		
Beaded Drapes						
Bowl, Footed	45.00	40.00	35.00	55.00		
Banana Bowl, Footed						
Rose Bowl, Footed	50.00	45.00	40.00	60.00		
Beaded Fan						
Bowl, Footed	40.00	45.00	36.00			
Rose Bowl, Footed	50.00	50.00	42.00			
Beaded Fleur De Lis						
Compote	50.00	50.00	40.00			
Rose Bowl	55.00	55.00	47.00			
Beaded Moon & Stars						
Bowl	70.00					
Beaded Ovals & Holly						
Spooner	90.00		65.00	85.00		

	Blue	Green	White	Vaseline/ Canary	Cranberry	Other
Beaded Ovals In Sand						
Pitcher	400.00	400.00				
Tumbler	95.00	90.00				
Butter	285.00	265.00				
Sugar	225.00	225.00				
Creamer	90.00	80.00				
Spooner	90.00	80.00				
Bowl, Master	75.00	70.00				
Bowl, Sauce	35.00	30.00				
Cruet	240.00	225.00				
Shakers, pair	100.00	90.00				
Toothpick Holder	200.00	190.00				
Nappy	55.00	45.00				
Beaded Star Medallion						
Shade		55.00	45.00			
Beaded Stars						
Plate	95.00					
Bowl	45.00	55.00	37.00			
Rose Bowl	60.00	60.00	42.00			
Advertising Bowl	240.00					
Advertising Plate	295.00					
Beads & Bark						
Vase, footed	75.00	70.00	60.00			
Beads & Curleycues						
Novelty Bowls, ftd.	48.00	46.00	40.00			
(Beatty) Honeycomb*						
Pitcher	195.00		150.00			
Tumbler	60.00		40.00			
Sugar	120.00		90.00			
Creamer	100.00		60.00			
Spooner	90.00		60.00			
Bowl, Master	55.00		45.00			
Bowl, Sauce	30.00		25.00			
Cruet	200.00		175.00			
Toothpick Holder	250.00		225.00			
Celery Vase	85.00		75.00			
Shakers, pair	80.00		65.00			
Mustard Pot	100.00		80.00			
Mug	55.00		40.00			
Individual cream/sugar set	165.00		135.00			
Butter	200.00		160.00			
Beatty Rib						
Pitcher	185.00		140.00			

	Blue	Green	White	Vaseline/ Canary	Cranberry	Other
Tumbler	50.00		35.00			
Butter	200.00		115.00			
Sugar	135.00		95.00			
Creamer	65.00		40.00			
Spooner	65.00		40.00			
Bowl, Master	55.00		35.00			
Bowl, Sauce	30.00		20.00			
Celery Vase	80.00		70.00			
Mug	55.00		40.00			
Ashtray, Cigar	85.00*					
Mustard Jar	150.00		110.00			
Nappy, various	40.00		30.00			
Shakers, pair	75.00		60.00			
Salt Dip	60.00		45.00			
Cracker Jar	120.00		90.00			
Sugar Shaker	125.00		100.00			
Finger Bowl	35.00		25.00			
Match Holder	50.00		35.00			
Toothpick	65.00		55.00			
Beatty Swirl						
Pitcher	180.00		120.00	190.00		
Tumbler	40.00		35.00	50.00		
Butter	170.00		150.00			
Sugar	130.00		90.00			
Creamer	75.00		60.00			
Spooner	75.00		60.00			
Bowl, Master	55.00		40.00			
Bowl, Sauce	30.00		21.00			
Celery Vase	80.00		60.00			
Mug	60.00		40.00	80.00		
Syrup	240.00		190.00	250.00		
Water Tray	90.00		70.00	95.00		
Berry Patch						
Novelty Bowl	50.00	45.00	35.00			
Blackberry						
Nappy	40.00	45.00	30.00			55.00 Amethyst
Blocked Thumbprint & Beads **(Fishscale & Beads)**						
Bowl	50.00	55.00	40.00			
Nappy	40.00	40.00	30.00			
Blooms & Blossoms						
Nappy, Handled	50.00	50.00	40.00			
Blossom & Palms						
Bowl	47.00	45.00	36.00			

	Blue	Green	White	Vaseline/ Canary	Cranberry	Other
Blossom & Web						
Bowl	70.00	70.00	45.00			
(Blown) Drape						
Pitcher	550.00	500.00	350.00		900.00	
Tumbler	185.00	175.00	155.00		315.00	
Barber Bottle	450.00	375.00	275.00			
(Blown) Twist						
Pitcher	550.00	500.00	350.00	525.00	900.00	
Tumbler	185.00	175.00	155.00	175.00	315.00	
Sugar Shaker	195.00	185.00	170.00	185.00	575.00	
Syrup	250.00		190.00		380.00	
Boggy Bayou						
Vase	40.00	37.00	30.00			60.00 Amethyst
Brideshead						
Pitcher	145.00*					
Tumbler	90.00*					
Butter	95.00					
Sugar	70.00					
Creamer	65.00					
Celery Vase	60.00					
Novelty Bowl	50.00					
Broken Pillar						
Compote	60.00			55.00		
Card Tray	70.00			65.00		
(from compote shape)						
(Bubble) Lattice						
Pitcher, various	270.00	260.00	210.00	265.00	750.00	
Tumbler, various	50.00	50.00	40.00	45.00	110.00	
Butter	200.00	180.00	145.00	195.00	700.00	
Sugar	100.00	80.00	70.00	95.00	420.00	
Creamer	60.00	50.00	50.00	55.00	150.00	
Spooner	60.00	50.00	50.00	55.00	195.00	
Bowl, Master	70.00	50.00	45.00	65.00	80.00	
Sauce	30.00	25.00	20.00	30.00	35.00	
Cruet, avg. pricing	175.00	160.00	135.00	170.00	400.00	
Syrup, various	200.00	180.00	160.00	190.00	750.00	
Sugar Shaker	225.00	210.00	185.00	215.00	290.00	
Toothpick holder	300.00	265.00	190.00	350.00	280.00 – 540.00	
Bride's Basket	120.00	95.00	70.00	125.00	225.00	
Finger Bowl	45.00	40.00	25.00	45.00	110.00	
Shakers, various	150.00	125.00	100.00	175.00	150.00 – 300.00	
Celery Vase					120.00	

	Blue	Green	White	Vaseline/ Canary	Cranberry	Other
Bulbous Base Coinspot						
Sugar Shaker	120.00		90.00		165.00	
Bullseye						
Bowl	50.00				65.00	
Water Bottle			160.00		250.00	
Shade	60.00		40.00			
Bushel Basket						
One shape, scarce	150.00	325.00	90.00			
Button Panels						
Bowl	45.00		35.00	50.00		
Rose Bowl	45.00		37.00	55.00		
Buttons & Braids						
Pitcher	180.00	170.00	125.00	275.00*	395.00	
Tumbler	45.00	40.00	30.00	80.00*	90.00	
Bowl	50.00	55.00	35.00		85.00	
Cabbage Leaf						
Novelty, Footed Bowl	80.00	65.00	50.00			
Calyx						
Vase	65.00		50.00	60.00		
Carousel						
Bowl	55.00	50.00	37.00			
Cane & Diamond Swirl						
Stemmed Tray	75.00			70.00		
Cashews						
Bowl	50.00	47.00	30.00			
Rose Bowl, rare	100.00	95.00	75.00			
Cherry Panels						
Novelty Bowl	75.00		60.00	70.00		
Chippendale						
Compote	65.00			75.00		
Basket	60.00			60.00		
Pitcher	120.00			135.00		
Tumbler	35.00			30.00		
Christmas Pearls						
Cruet	295.00	275.00	350.00*			
Shakers, pair	150.00	135.00	175.00*			

	Blue	Green	White	Vaseline/ Canary	Cranberry	Other	
Christmas Snowflake*							
Pitcher, either	675.00		500.00		950.00		
Tumbler, average	110.00		90.00		125.00		
Chrysanthemum Base Swirl							
Pitcher	395.00		345.00		850.00		
Tumbler	90.00		70.00		120.00		
Butter	325.00		295.00		500.00		
Sugar	200.00		175.00		350.00		
Creamer	95.00		70.00		395.00		
Spooner	95.00		70.00		200.00		
Bowl, Master	55.00		45.00		120.00		
Bowl, Sauce	35.00		30.00		50.00		
Cruet	225.00		175.00		475.00		
Syrup	200.00		175.00		495.00		
Sugar Shaker	200.00		175.00		265.00		
Toothpick Holder	95.00		70.00		300.00		
Shakers, pair	125.00		100.00		295.00		
Finger Bowl	45.00		35.00		140.00		
Celery Vase	135.00		110.00		200.00		
Straw Holder w/lid	500.00		400.00		1,200.00		
Mustard Pot	150.00		120.00		225.00		
Chrysanthemum Swirl Variant							
Pitcher, rare	375.00		265.00		900.00	400.00	Teal
Tumbler, rare	90.00		60.00		100.00		
Circled Scroll							
Pitcher	475.00	425.00	400.00				
Tumbler	90.00	85.00	70.00				
Butter	465.00	350.00	295.00				
Sugar	250.00	225.00	200.00				
Creamer	175.00	165.00	125.00				
Spooner	175.00	165.00	125.00				
Bowl, Master	165.00	150.00	120.00				
Bowl, Sauce	55.00	50.00	40.00				
Cruet	395.00	375.00	350.00				
Shakers, pair	300.00	295.00	245.00				
Jelly Compote	150.00	140.00	125.00				
Cleopatra's Fan (Northwood Shell)							
Vase, novelty	65.00	75.00					
Coinspot* (includes variants — prices averaged)							
Pitcher	260.00	245.00	165.00	190.00	390.00	200.00	Rubina
Tumbler	40.00	35.00	30.00	36.00	90.00	75.00	Rubina
Bowl, Master	47.00	40.00	30.00		70.00		
Bowl, Sauce	30.00	25.00	18.00		40.00		

	Blue	Green	White	Vaseline/ Canary	Cranberry	Other	
Syrup	165.00	150.00	135.00		395.00	300.00	Rubina
Cruet, various	250.00	230.00	100.00	240.00	375.00	400.00	Rubina
Shakers, each	135.00	95.00	70.00	90.00	195.00		
Compote	60.00	45.00	40.00				
Sugar Shaker	100.00	95.00	75.00	100.00	375.00	250.00	Rubina
Novelty Bowls	60.00	55.00	40.00		75.00		
Celery Vase	125.00	110.00	90.00	120.00	175.00		
Tumble-up	150.00	140.00	120.00		275.00		
Toothpick Holder	265.00	250.00	140.00	230.00	275.00	295.00	Rubina
Barber Bottle	175.00	170.00	130.00		300.00		
Pickle Castor	295.00		200.00		750.00		
Lamp (from syrup)	295.00		240.00		900.00		
Perfume	65.00	75.00	60.00				

Colonial Stairsteps

	Blue	Green	White	Vaseline/ Canary	Cranberry	Other	
Creamer	100.00						
Sugar	100.00						
Toothpick Holder	195.00						

Compass

	Blue	Green	White	Vaseline/ Canary	Cranberry	Other	
Plate, rare	250.00	225.00					

Concave Columns

	Blue	Green	White	Vaseline/ Canary	Cranberry	Other	
Vase	100.00		75.00	95.00			

Consolidated Crisscross

	Blue	Green	White	Vaseline/ Canary	Cranberry	Other	
Pitcher			550.00		950.00		
Tumbler			100.00		115.00		
Sugar			325.00		365.00		
Butter			425.00		725.00		
Creamer			250.00		365.00		
Spooner			225.00		285.00		
Bowl, Master			110.00		185.00		
Bowl, Sauce			50.00		70.00		
Shakers, each			90.00		100.00	165.00	Rubina
Cruet			275.00		795.00		
Sugar Shaker			310.00		550.00	660.00	Rubina
Syrup			325.00		825.00	700.00	Rubina
Finger Bowl			90.00		120.00		
Celery Vase			135.00		175.00		
Mustard Pot			150.00		195.00		
Toothpick Holder			195.00		500.00		
Ivy Ball			300.00*		700.00		

Constellation (Seafoam)

	Blue	Green	White	Vaseline/ Canary	Cranberry	Other	
Compote	275.00		200.00				

Contessa

	Blue	Green	White	Vaseline/ Canary	Cranberry	Other	
Basket, Handled	60.00			75.00		250.00	Amber

	Blue	Green	White	Vaseline/ Canary	Cranberry	Other	
Pitcher	125.00						
Breakfast Set, ftd., 2 pc.	155.00					325.00	Amber
						350.00	Amber
Coral							
Bowl	45.00	40.00	30.00	40.00			
Corn Vase*							
Fancy Vase	200.00	295.00	125.00	185.00			
Cornucopia							
Handled Vase	75.00		57.00				
Coronation							
Pitcher	195.00			185.00			
Tumbler	40.00			40.00			
Crown Jewels							
Pitcher	195.00						
Tumbler	55.00						
Curtain Call							
Caster Set – rare						500.00	Cobalt
Curtain Optic							
Pitcher, various	200.00	200.00	150.00	185.00			
Tumbler, various	50.00	45.00	40.00	45.00			
Guest Set, 2 pc.	95.00	100.00	80.00	100.00			
Daffodils							
Pitcher	900.00	950.00	600.00	850.00	1,350.00		
Tumbler, rare	395.00	350.00	300.00	395.00	550.00		
Oil Lamp	300.00	295.00	200.00	275.00	325.00		
Dahlia Twist							
Vase	65.00	60.00	50.00				
Epergne	150.00	140.00	100.00				
Daisy Block							
Rowboat, 4 sizes		80.00*	70.00*				
Daisy & Button							
Lifeboat				75.00			
Bun Tray				150.00			
Bowl, novelty				65.00			
Daisy In Crisscross							
Pitcher	300.00				450.00		
Tumbler	60.00				100.00		
Syrup	265.00				475.00		

	Blue	Green	White	Vaseline/Canary	Cranberry	Other
Daisy Dear						
Bowl	45.00	40.00	30.00			
Daisy & Fern*						
Pitcher, 3 shapes	290.00	285.00	190.00		300.00 – 750.00	
Tumbler	45.00	55.00	30.00		90.00	
Butter	225.00	250.00	175.00		285.00	
Sugar	100.00	120.00	75.00		250.00	
Creamer	75.00	90.00	60.00		425.00	
Vase	140.00	140.00	90.00		190.00	
Spooner	75.00	85.00	50.00		395.00	
Bowl, Master	80.00	95.00	55.00		120.00	
Bowl, Sauce	40.00	45.00	26.00		45.00	
Sugar shaker	195.00	220.00	165.00		265.00	
Syrup, various, avg.	225.00	215.00	185.00		240.00 – 540.00	
Toothpick Holder	155.00	170.00	110.00		200.00	
Shakers, pair	300.00	260.00	175.00		295.00	
Mustard Pot	95.00	110.00	75.00		150.00	
Cruet	200.00	175.00	135.00		510.00	
Perfume Bottle	170.00	195.00	120.00		250.00	
Night Lamp	220.00	240.00	160.00		310.00	
Pickle Caster	315.00	325.00	245.00		425.00	
Barber Bottle					495.00	
Rose Bowl					110.00	
Daisy Intaglio						
Basket			150.00			
Bowl			85.00			
Plate			100.00			
Daisy May (Leaf Rays)						
Bon-Bon or Nappy	40.00	45.00	28.00			
Daisy & Plume						
Bowl, footed	50.00	45.00	35.00			
Daisy Wreath						
Bowl, rare	150.00*					
Dandelion						
Mug, rare	700.00*					
Desert Garden						
Bowl	45.00	40.00	30.00			
Diamond & Daisy						
Bowl, Novelty	40.00	45.00	35.00			
Basket, Handled	50.00	60.00	40.00			

	Blue	Green	White	Vaseline/ Canary	Cranberry	Other
Diamond Maple Leaf						
Novelty, Handled	40.00	50.00	30.00	45.00		
Bowl, Handled	75.00	70.00	50.00			
Diamond Optic						
Compote	50.00		40.00			
Stemmed Cardtray	60.00		50.00			
Diamond & Oval Thumbprint						
Vase	40.00	45.00	30.00			
Diamond Point						
Vase	40.00	45.00	30.00			
Diamond Point Columns						
Vase, rare	200.00	200.00	150.00			
Diamond Point & Fleur De Lis						
Bowl, Novelty	50.00	55.00	40.00			
Diamond Spearhead						
Pitcher	700.00	600.00	395.00	475.00		
Tumbler	110.00	90.00	50.00	80.00		
Goblet	165.00	150.00	100.00	140.00		
Butter	500.00	575.00	395.00	495.00		
Sugar	250.00	225.00	175.00	250.00		
Creamer	195.00	210.00	165.00	195.00		
Spooner	165.00	200.00	155.00	170.00		
Bowl, Master	175.00	180.00	110.00	165.00		
Bowl, Sauce	50.00	55.00	30.00	40.00		
Toothpick Holder	150.00	125.00	100.00	130.00		
Mug	175.00	185.00	90.00	150.00		
Syrup	650.00	700.00	550.00	625.00		
Celery Vase	250.00	250.00	150.00	250.00		
Shakers, pair	150.00	175.00	130.00	165.00		
Jelly Compote	195.00	150.00	125.00	165.00		
Cup & Saucer Set				250.00		
Tall Compote	400.00	395.00	300.00	395.00		
Tall Creamer	200.00			200.00		
Oil Bottle	100.00			90.00		
Diamond Stem						
Vase			40.00	55.00		
Diamond Wave						
Pitcher w/Lid					165.00	
Tumbler					40.00	
Diamonds						
Pitcher, 2 shapes					400.00	275.00 Rubina

	Blue	Green	White	Vaseline/ Canary	Cranberry	Other
Cruet					350.00	
Vase, 6" decorated			75.00			
Dolly Madison						
Pitcher	395.00	400.00	310.00			
Tumbler	80.00	95.00	60.00			
Butter	325.00	350.00	275.00			
Sugar	150.00	160.00	110.00			
Creamer	90.00	100.00	75.00			
Spooner	80.00	90.00	60.00			
Bowl, Master	60.00	70.00	55.00			
Bowl, Sauce	30.00	35.00	25.00			
Dolphin*						
Compote	65.00		45.00	60.00		
Dolphin & Herons						
Compote, Footed Novelty	95.00		80.00	120.00		
Tray, Footed Novelty	90.00		75.00			
Dolphin Petticoat						
Candlestick, pair	175.00		125.00	165.00		
Double Greek Key						
Pitcher	375.00		325.00			
Tumbler	80.00		65.00			
Butter	300.00		250.00			
Sugar	175.00		140.00			
Creamer	100.00		75.00			
Spooner	100.00		75.00			
Bowl, Master	75.00		60.00			
Bowl, Sauce	40.00		30.00			
Celery Vase	165.00		135.00			
Pickle Tray	150.00		95.00			
Shakers, pair	225.00		185.00			
Mustard Pot	200.00		155.00			
Toothpick Holder	250.00		195.00			
Double Stemmed Rose						
Bowl, very rare	250.00	200.00	150.00			
Dragon Lady						
Rose Bowl	45.00	40.00	35.00			
Novelty Bowl	40.00	35.00	30.00			
Vase	50.00	45.00	38.00			
Drapery, Northwood's						
Pitcher	250.00		220.00			
Tumbler	70.00		55.00			
Butter	195.00		175.00			

	Blue	Green	White	Vaseline/ Canary	Cranberry	Other
Sugar	135.00		120.00			
Creamer	90.00		80.00			
Spooner	80.00		70.00			
Bowl, Master	110.00		75.00			
Bowl, Sauce	40.00		30.00			
Rose Bowl	90.00		75.00			
Duchess						
Pitcher	175.00		150.00	175.00		
Tumbler	35.00		27.00	30.00		
Butter	175.00		150.00	165.00		
Sugar	100.00		80.00	100.00		
Creamer	65.00		45.00	60.00		
Spooner	65.00		50.00	65.00		
Bowl, Master	95.00		65.00	80.00		
Bowl, Sauce	35.00		25.00	30.00		
Toothpick Holder	150.00		115.00	150.00		
Cruet	200.00		160.00	195.00		
Lampshade	95.00		75.00			
Dugan's Diamond Compass						
Bowl, rare			90.00			
Dugan Jack-in-the-Pulpit						
Vase, 4½"	50.00		35.00			
Hex Base Vase, 7½"	60.00					
Ellipse & Diamond						
Pitcher					500.00*	
Tumbler					115.00*	
English Spool						
Vase				65.00		
Estate						
Vase	65.00	85.00	40.00			
Everglades						
Pitcher	460.00			495.00		
Tumbler	85.00			90.00		
Butter	360.00			375.00		
Sugar	195.00			200.00		
Creamer	150.00			150.00		
Spooner	150.00			150.00		
Oval Bowl, Master	185.00			195.00		
Oval Bowl, Sauce	40.00			40.00		
Cruet	475.00			495.00		
Shakers, pair	275.00			280.00		
Jelly Compote	140.00	165.00		140.00		

	Blue	Green	White	Vaseline/ Canary	Cranberry	Other
Fan						
Pitcher	295.00	290.00	200.00			
Tumbler	35.00	30.00	20.00			
Butter	395.00	385.00	220.00			
Sugar	200.00	185.00	150.00			
Creamer	120.00	110.00	85.00			
Spooner	120.00	110.00	85.00			
Bowl, Master	75.00	70.00	65.00			
Bowl, Sauce	30.00	30.00	25.00			
Gravy Boat	45.00	48.00	40.00			
Novelty Bowls	40.00	40.00	30.00			
Whimsey Bowls	50.00	50.00	40.00			
Fancy Fantails						
Bowl	40.00	45.00	25.00	40.00		
Rose Bowl	45.00	50.00	30.00	45.00		
Feathers						
Vase	35.00	32.00	26.00			
Whimsey Bowl, rare			200.00*			
Fenton Drapery						
Pitcher	420.00*	400.00*	290.00*			
Tumbler	65.00*	55.00*	40.00*			
Fern						
Pitcher, various	250.00		175.00		700.00 – 800.00	
Tumbler	45.00		40.00		100.00	
Butter	250.00		220.00		375.00	
Sugar	200.00		170.00		230.00	
Bowl, Master	100.00		75.00		125.00	
Bowl, Sauce	50.00		35.00		55.00	
Sugar Shaker, various	100.00		75.00		525.00	
Syrup	275.00		200.00		595.00	
Cruet	200.00		200.00		495.00	
Shakers, pair	160.00		100.00		150.00	
Celery Vase	125.00		90.00		145.00	
Mustard Pot	140.00		115.00		165.00	
Toothpick Holder, rare	350.00		190.00		400.00 – 500.00	
Finger Bowl	65.00		45.00		100.00	
Barber Bottle	150.00		100.00		295.00	
Creamer	125.00		90.00		150.00	
Spooner	125.00		90.00		140.00	
Finecut & Roses						
Rose Bowl, rare	65.00	75.00	50.00			
Novelty Bowls	45.00	50.00	40.00			
Fish In The Sea						
Vase	300.00	295.00	270.00			

	Blue	Green	White	Vaseline/Canary	Cranberry	Other
Vase Whimsey	95.00	90.00	70.00			

Fishnet

	Blue	Green	White	Vaseline/Canary	Cranberry	Other
Epergne	165.00		125.00			185.00 Emerald
(one shape, 2 pc.)						

Fishscale & Beads

	Blue	Green	White	Vaseline/Canary	Cranberry	Other
Bowl	40.00		28.00			

Flora

	Blue	Green	White	Vaseline/Canary	Cranberry	Other
Pitcher	495.00		400.00	475.00		
Tumbler	85.00		60.00	80.00		
Butter	275.00		175.00	250.00		
Sugar	135.00		100.00	125.00		
Creamer	100.00		75.00	90.00		
Spooner	100.00		90.00	100.00		
Bowl, Master	100.00		75.00	95.00		
Bowl, Sauce	50.00		30.00	40.00		
Cruet	750.00		450.00	600.00		
Toothpick Holder	475.00		300.00	400.00		
Syrup	400.00		300.00	395.00		
Shakers, pair	395.00		295.00	375.00		
Jelly Compote	150.00		110.00	140.00		
Celery Vase	125.00		90.00	100.00		
Novelty Bowl	65.00		40.00	55.00		

Floral Eyelet*

	Blue	Green	White	Vaseline/Canary	Cranberry	Other
Pitcher	500.00*		400.00*		850.00*	
Tumbler	100.00*		85.00*		250.00*	

Fluted Bars & Beads

	Blue	Green	White	Vaseline/Canary	Cranberry	Other
Rose Bowl	50.00	45.00	40.00			
Novelty Bowl	55.00	50.00	45.00			
Vase Novelty	60.00	55.00	50.00			

Fluted Scrolls (Klondyke)

	Blue	Green	White	Vaseline/Canary	Cranberry	Other
Pitcher	240.00		165.00	200.00		
Tumbler	90.00		40.00	75.00		
Butter	175.00		150.00	170.00		
Sugar	130.00		90.00	100.00		
Spooner	75.00		50.00	60.00		
Creamer	75.00		50.00	70.00		
Bowl, Master	75.00		55.00	70.00		
Bowl, Sauce	30.00		25.00	30.00		
Cruet	185.00		160.00	175.00		
Shakers, pair	95.00		70.00	80.00		
Epergne, small	120.00		90.00	125.00		
Rose Bowl	135.00		85.00	120.00		
Novelty Bowl	50.00		40.00	50.00		
Puff Box	65.00		50.00	60.00		

Note: A variant called Fluted Scrolls with Flower Band is priced the same as above.

	Blue	Green	White	Vaseline/ Canary	Cranberry	Other	
Fluted Scrolls With Vine							
Vase, Footed	75.00		45.00	85.00			
Frosted Leaf & Basketweave							
Butter	275.00			250.00			
Sugar	175.00			160.00			
Creamer	150.00			135.00			
Spooner	140.00			120.00			
Gonterman (Adonis) Hob							
Cruet						425.00	Amber
Gonterman (Adonis) Swirl							
Pitcher	400.00					375.00	Amber
Tumbler	90.00					75.00	Amber
Butter	390.00					340.00	Amber
Sugar	250.00					210.00	Amber
Creamer	175.00					125.00	Amber
Spooner	150.00					120.00	Amber
Bowl, Master	95.00					85.00	Amber
Bowl, Sauce	50.00					50.00	Amber
Cruet	400.00					375.00	Amber
Celery Vase	210.00					195.00	Amber
Syrup	400.00					375.00	Amber
Shade	100.00					100.00	Amber
Toothpick Holder	300.00					195.00	Amber
Grape & Cable							
Centerpiece Bowl	275.00	265.00	200.00	245.00			
Bon-Bon				400.00			
Grape & Cherry							
Bowl	70.00		55.00				
Grapevine Cluster							
Vase, Footed	75.00		60.00				
Greek Key & Ribs							
Bowl	60.00	55.00	40.00				
Greek Key & Scales							
Novelty Bowl	85.00	75.00	60.00				
Heart-Handle Open O's							
Ring Tray	95.00	85.00	65.00				
Hearts & Clubs							
Bowl, Footed	55.00	50.00	40.00				

	Blue	Green	White	Vaseline/Canary	Cranberry	Other
Hearts & Flowers						
Bowl	75.00		60.00			
Compote	150.00		100.00			
Heatherbloom						
Vase	35.00	32.00	20.00			
Herringbone						
Pitcher	575.00		475.00		725.00	
Tumbler	100.00		60.00		150.00	
Cruet	295.00		220.00		685.00	
Heron & Peacock*						
Mug	70.00		60.00			
Hilltop Vines						
Novelty Chalice	65.00	60.00	40.00			
Hobnail, Hobbs						
Pitcher , 5 Sizes	250.00 – 350.00		150.00 – 250.00	200.00 – 300.00	350.00 – 550.00	250.00 – 400.00 Rubina
Tumbler	70.00		50.00	70.00		100.00 Rubina
Butter	275.00		190.00	225.00		
Sugar	200.00		135.00	165.00		
Creamer	90.00		100.00	95.00		
Spooner	90.00		100.00	95.00		
Bowl, Master, square	90.00		75.00	95.00		
Bowl, Sauce, square	35.00		30.00	30.00		
Cruet	200.00		200.00	190.00		
Syrup	225.00		200.00	210.00		
Finger Bowl	65.00		50.00	55.00		350.00 Rubina
Barber Bottle	145.00		125.00	130.00		
Celery Vase	160.00		120.00	100.00		225.00 Rubina
Water Tray	175.00		110.00	140.00		
Bride's Basket	450.00			410.00	500.00	500.00 Rubina
Lemonade Set, Complete	600.00				700.00	
Hobnail, Northwood's						
Pitcher			100.00			
Tumbler			30.00			
Butter			130.00			
Sugar			100.00			
Creamer			60.00			
Spooner			60.00			
Bowl, Master			55.00			
Bowl, Sauce			30.00			
Mug			85.00			
Celery Vase			95.00			
Breakfast Set, 2 piece set			135.00			

	Blue	Green	White	Vaseline/ Canary	Cranberry	Other	
Hobnail 4-Footed							
Butter			155.00	175.00		210.00	Cobalt
Sugar			80.00	110.00		135.00	Cobalt
Creamer			70.00	85.00		90.00	Cobalt
Spooner			70.00	85.00		90.00	Cobalt
Hobnail & Panelled Thumbprint							
Pitcher	300.00		150.00	275.00			
Tumbler	75.00		45.00	65.00			
Butter	185.00		140.00	170.00			
Sugar	115.00		90.00	85.00			
Creamer	85.00		60.00	65.00			
Spooner	85.00		65.00	70.00			
Bowl, Master	75.00		60.00	65.00			
Bowl, Sauce	35.00		26.00	32.00			
Hobnail In Square* (Vesta)							
Pitcher			220.00				
Tumbler			35.00				
Butter			185.00				
Sugar			130.00				
Creamer			100.00				
Spooner			90.00				
Bowl, Master			70.00				
Bowl, Sauce			27.00				
Celery Vase			130.00				
Shakers, pair			90.00				
Compote, various			95.00				
Barber Bottle			120.00				
Bowl, with stand	150.00		100.00				
Holly							
Bowl			75.00				
Honeycomb							
Vase	75.00*						
Honeycomb (Blown)							
Pitcher	300.00		210.00		475.00	425.00	Amber
Tumbler	75.00		45.00		90.00	65.00	Amber
Cracker Jar	310.00		245.00		395.00	400.00	Amber
Syrup	295.00		270.00		410.00	450.00	Amber
Barber Bottle	170.00		110.00		170.00	190.00	Amber
Honeycomb & Clover							
Pitcher	395.00	350.00	275.00				
Tumbler	100.00	80.00	60.00				
Butter	365.00	350.00	270.00				
Sugar	290.00	275.00	145.00				
Creamer	150.00	140.00	110.00				

	Blue	Green	White	Vaseline/ Canary	Cranberry	Other
Spooner	150.00	140.00	110.00			
Bowl, Master	85.00	80.00	60.00			
Bowl, Sauce	40.00	35.00	30.00			
Bowl, Novelty	70.00	70.00	60.00			

Horse Chestnut

	Blue	Green	White	Vaseline/ Canary	Cranberry	Other
Blown Vase				95.00*		

Idyll

	Blue	Green	White	Vaseline/ Canary	Cranberry	Other
Pitcher	375.00	360.00	300.00			
Tumbler	90.00	85.00	70.00			
Butter	350.00	370.00	295.00			
Sugar	170.00	195.00	150.00			
Creamer	140.00	130.00	80.00			
Spooner	140.00	130.00	75.00			
Bowl, Master	60.00	60.00	40.00			
Bowl, Sauce	30.00	30.00	20.00			
Toothpick Holder	395.00	310.00	270.00			
Cruet	210.00	200.00	170.00			
Shakers, pair	115.00	100.00	90.00			
Tray	120.00	110.00	90.00			
Bowl, 6" – 7"	40.00	45.00	30.00			

Inside Ribbing

	Blue	Green	White	Vaseline/ Canary	Cranberry	Other
Bowl, Master	65.00		40.00	75.00		
Bowl, Sauce	30.00		20.00	35.00		
Butter	225.00		150.00	240.00		
Sugar	110.00		90.00	120.00		
Spooner	75.00		60.00	80.00		
Creamer	75.00		60.00	80.00		
Pitcher	275.00		160.00	280.00		
Tumbler	60.00		30.00	65.00		
Celery Vase	55.00		35.00	60.00		
Syrup	150.00		95.00	140.00		
Jelly Compote	65.00		30.00	60.00		
Toothpick Holder	200.00		160.00	195.00		
Cruet	135.00		90.00	130.00		
Shakers, pair	100.00		70.00	90.00		
Tray	50.00		30.00	50.00		
Rose Bowl	75.00					

Intaglio

	Blue	Green	White	Vaseline/ Canary	Cranberry	Other
Pitcher	225.00		135.00			
Tumbler	110.00		65.00			
Butter	485.00		260.00			
Sugar	160.00		95.00			
Creamer	85.00		50.00			
Spooner	90.00		60.00			
Bowl, Master, Ftd.	220.00		90.00			
Bowl, Sauce, Ftd.	35.00		20.00			

	Blue	Green	White	Vaseline/ Canary	Cranberry	Other	
Shakers, pair	95.00		75.00				
Jelly Compote	60.00		45.00				
Novelty Bowl	50.00		30.00	65.00			
Cruet	195.00		140.00	300.00*			

Intaglio, Dugan's

	Blue	Green	White	Vaseline/ Canary	Cranberry	Other	
Bowl, 7" – 10"			120.00				
Compote, 5" – 7"			100.00				
Compote, 8" – 11"			150.00				
Nappy, 6" – 9"			75.00				
Plate, 11"			135.00				

Note: These items are all goofus on crystal with opalescent treatment.

Interior Panel

	Blue	Green	White	Vaseline/ Canary	Cranberry	Other	
Fan Vase	55.00	50.00	35.00	55.00		75.00	Amber
						80.00	Amethyst

Interior Swirl

	Blue	Green	White	Vaseline/ Canary	Cranberry	Other	
Rose Bowl	100.00		55.00	95.00			

Inverted Coindot

	Blue	Green	White	Vaseline/ Canary	Cranberry	Other	
Tumbler		60.00	35.00				
Rose Bowl			55.00	90.00			

Inverted Fan & Feather*

	Blue	Green	White	Vaseline/ Canary	Cranberry	Other	
Pitcher	750.00		600.00				
Tumbler	90.00		65.00				
Butter	500.00		390.00				
Sugar	300.00		235.00				
Creamer	225.00		165.00				
Spooner	225.00		165.00				
Rose Bowl		285.00*		150.00			
Bowl, Master	300.00		190.00				
Bowl, Sauce	85.00		40.00				
Cruet, rare	495.00						
Shakers, pair, rare	350.00						
Jelly Compote, rare	250.00		175.00				
Toothpick, rare	500.00						
Punchbowl, rare	650.00						
Punch Cup, rare	45.00						
Novelty Bowl, v. rare		250.00*		285.00*			
Spittoon Whimsey	350.00*		270.00*	340.00*			
Plate, very rare				500.00*			
Vase Whimsey, rare	200.00*	200.00*	150.00*				

Iris With Meander

	Blue	Green	White	Vaseline/ Canary	Cranberry	Other	
Pitcher	390.00	375.00	285.00	320.00			
Tumbler	80.00	75.00	60.00	75.00			
Butter	295.00	275.00	220.00	275.00			

	Blue	Green	White	Vaseline/Canary	Cranberry	Other
Sugar	160.00	145.00	90.00	160.00		
Creamer	95.00	80.00	65.00	75.00		
Spooner	95.00	80.00	60.00	80.00		
Bowl, Master	200.00	145.00	70.00	150.00		
Bowl, Sauce, 2 sizes	40.00 – 50.00	25.00 – 35.00	18.00 – 24.00	40.00		
Toothpick Holder	135.00	120.00	70.00	110.00		
Shakers, pair	210.00	200.00	165.00	190.00		
Cruet	465.00	395.00	275.00	395.00		450.00 Amber
Jelly Compote	55.00	50.00	35.00	45.00		
Vase, tall	60.00	55.00	40.00	60.00		
Pickle Dish	85.00	75.00	55.00	75.00		
Plate	145.00	140.00	110.00	135.00		
Jackson						
Pitcher	460.00		375.00	430.00		
Tumbler	80.00		65.00	80.00		
Butter	210.00		130.00	200.00		
Sugar	120.00		90.00	115.00		
Creamer	80.00		60.00	70.00		
Spooner	80.00		60.00	70.00		
Bowl, Master	85.00		70.00	75.00		
Bowl, Sauce	35.00		20.00	30.00		
Cruet	185.00		160.00	175.00		
Epergne, small	170.00		95.00	135.00		
Candy Dish	55.00		35.00	50.00		
Powder Jar	70.00		40.00	65.00		
Jefferson Shield						
Bowl	125.00*	135.00*	90.00*			
Jefferson Spool						
Vase	50.00	45.00	40.00			
Vase Whimsey	55.00	50.00	45.00			
Jefferson Stripe						
Vase, Jack-in-the-Pulpit	60.00	65.00	45.00			
Jefferson Wheel						
Bowl	55.00	50.00	40.00			
Jewel & Fan						
Bowl	60.00	55.00	45.00			
Banana Bowl	110.00	125.00				
Jewel & Flower						
Pitcher	675.00		310.00	500.00		
Tumbler	90.00		65.00	80.00		
Butter	365.00		210.00	325.00		
Sugar	200.00		125.00	190.00		
Creamer	115.00		90.00	150.00		

	Blue	Green	White	Vaseline/ Canary	Cranberry	Other
Spooner	110.00		85.00	125.00		
Bowl, Master	70.00		50.00	70.00		
Bowl, Sauce	35.00		25.00	35.00		
Cruet	675.00		310.00	625.00		
Shakers, pair	160.00		105.00	150.00		
Novelty Bowl	50.00		30.00	50.00		
Jewelled Heart						
Pitcher	395.00	295.00	175.00			
Tumbler	80.00	65.00	40.00			
Butter	325.00	295.00	200.00			
Sugar	195.00	180.00	125.00			
Creamer	160.00	150.00	95.00			
Spooner	160.00	150.00	95.00			
Bowl, Master	65.00	60.00	50.00			
Bowl, Sauce	30.00	25.00	20.00			
Cruet	400.00	400.00	300.00			
Novelty Bowl	45.00	40.00	30.00			
Plate, small	70.00	65.00	50.00			
Compote	150.00	150.00	100.00			
Toothpick	250.00	230.00	190.00			
Sugar Shaker	350.00	325.00	275.00			
Syrup	500.00	475.00	395.00			
Shakers, pair	350.00	325.00	275.00			
Condiment Set (4 pieces, complete)	1,000.00	1,000.00	750.00			
Tray	250.00	225.00	175.00			
Jewels & Drapery						
Novelty Bowl	55.00	50.00	35.00			
Vase (from bowl)	50.00	45.00	30.00			
Jolly Bear						
Bowl	125.00	120.00	100.00			
Keyhole						
Bowl, scarce	85.00	90.00	65.00			
Lady Caroline						
Creamer	60.00			60.00		
Sugar	56.00			55.00		
Basket	65.00			60.00		
Whimsey, 3 handled	75.00			70.00		
Lady Chippendale						
Compote, Tall						90.00 Cobalt
Late Coinspot						
Pitcher	150.00	140.00	110.00			
Tumbler	40.00	35.00	27.00			

	Blue	Green	White	Vaseline/ Canary	Cranberry	Other	
Lattice & Daisy							
Tumbler, scarce	75.00		60.00				
Lattice Medallions							
Bowl	55.00	50.00	45.00				
Lattice & Points							
Hat Shape			60.00				
Vase			70.00				
Bowl, Novelty			55.00				
Laura (Single Flower Framed)							
Bowl, scarce	55.00	50.00	36.00				
Plate, ruffled, rare		150.00*	125.00*				
Nappy, scarce	60.00	55.00	40.00				
Leaf & Beads							
Bowl, Ftd. or Dome	60.00	55.00	40.00				
Rose Bowl	75.00	70.00	50.00				
Bowl, Whimsey	70.00	60.00	45.00				
Leaf Chalice							
Novelty compote	100.00	115.00	65.00	90.00		175.00	Cobalt
(found in several shapes from same mould)							
Leaf & Diamonds							
Bowl	50.00		30.00				
Leaf Mold							
Pitcher					520.00		
Tumbler					100.00		
Butter					410.00		
Sugar					285.00		
Creamer					170.00		
Spooner					160.00		
Bowl, Master					130.00		
Bowl, Sauce					50.00		
Syrup					375.00		
Sugar Shaker					350.00		
Celery Vase					320.00		
Shakers, pair					550.00		
Cruet					630.00		
Toothpick Holder					475.00		
Lined Heart							
Vase	42.00	40.00	32.00				
Linking Rings							
Bowl	60.00						

	Blue	Green	White	Vaseline/ Canary	Cranberry	Other
Pitcher	120.00					
Little Nell						
Vase	40.00	35.00	22.00			
Little Swan* (Pastel Swan)						
Novelty, 2 sizes	85.00	90.00	50.00	85.00		
Lords & Ladies						
Creamer	65.00					
Open Sugar	70.00					
Butter	90.00					
Lorna						
Vase	40.00		30.00	342.00		
Lustre Flute						
Pitcher	375.00		320.00			
Tumbler	95.00		60.00			
Butter	495.00		275.00			
Sugar	265.00		180.00			
Creamer	140.00		115 00			
Spooner	140.00		115.00			
Bowl, Master	275.00		220.00			
Bowl, Sauce	50.00		35.00			
Custard Cup	40.00		30.00			
Vase	60.00		47.00			
Many Loops						
Bowl	50.00	48.00	39.00			
Many Ribs (Model Flint)						
Vase	40.00		30.00	40.00		
Maple Leaf						
Jelly Compote	110.00	100.00	70.00	100.00		
Novelty Chalice	85.00	90.00	65.00	85.00		
Mary Ann						
Vase, rare	95.00		70.00			100.00 Amethyst
May Basket						
Basket Shape	80.00	75.00	60.00			
Meander						
Novelty Bowl	60.00	55.00	37.00			
Melon Optic Swirl						
Bowl, rare	80.00*	90.00*	60.00*	85.00*		

	Blue	Green	White	Vaseline/ Canary	Cranberry	Other
Melon Swirl						
Pitcher	450.00					
Tumbler	75.00					
Milky Way (Country Kitchen Vt.)						
Bowl, rare Millersburg			300.00*			
Miniature Epergne						
Epergne, one lily	150.00			150.00		
Netted Roses						
Bowl	70.00		50.00			
Plate	120.00		100.00			
Northern Star						
Bowl	65.00	60.00	45.00			
Plate	100.00	95.00	60.00			
Banana Bowl	75.00	70.00	50.00			
Northwood Block						
Novelty Bowl	50.00	45.00	30.00	45.00		
Celery Vase	60.00	60.00	40.00	55.00		
Northwood Stripe						
Vase	90.00	85.00	65.00	85.00		
Northwood's Many Ribs						
Vase	65.00	60.00	50.00	60.00		
Ocean Shell						
Novelty, Ftd., 3 variations	85.00	80.00	60.00			
Old Man Winter						
Basket, small	75.00	100.00	60.00			
Basket, large, Footed	150.00		95.00			
Opal Open* (Beaded Panels)						
Ring Bowl, Handled	90.00	85.00	60.00	85.00		
Bowl, Novelty	50.00	55.00	30.00	50.00		
Vase, Novelty	40.00	40.00	30.00	40.00		
Rose Bowl, Novelty	50.00	60.00	35.00	50.00		
Opal Spiral						
Sugar	350.00*					
Tumbler	90.00*					
Overlapping Leaves (Leaf Tiers)						
Bowl, Footed	65.00	70.00	40.00			
Plate, Footed	120.00	110.00	95.00			
Rose Bowl, Footed	70.00	75.00	45.00			

	Blue	Green	White	Vaseline/ Canary	Cranberry	Other
Over-All Hob						
Pitcher	220.00		155.00	195.00		
Tumbler	60.00		30.00	50.00		
Butter	240.00		165.00	220.00		
Sugar	175.00		95.00	150.00		
Creamer	95.00		45.00	85.00		
Spooner	95.00		50.00	85.00		
Bowl, Master	75.00		35.00	65.00		
Bowl, Sauce	30.00		25.00	28.00		
Toothpick Holder	195.00		135.00	185.00		
Celery Vase	75.00		50.00	70.00		
Finger Bowl	55.00		35.00	55.00		
Mug	70.00		50.00	75.00		
Palisades						
Vase, Novelty	50.00	45.00	35.00	55.00		
Bowl, Novelty	45.00	50.00	35.00	50.00		
Palm & Scroll						
Bowl, Footed	65.00	60.00	40.00	60.00		
Rose Bowl, Footed	75.00	70.00	50.00	70.00		
Palm Beach						
Pitcher	450.00			470.00		
Tumbler	90.00			100.00		
Butter	300.00			285.00		
Sugar	200.00			220.00		
Creamer	140.00			135.00		
Spooner	140.00			145.00		
Bowl, Master	85.00			80.00		
Bowl, Sauce, 2 sizes	40.00			45.00		
Jelly Compote	175.00			195.00		
Nappy, Handled, rare				425.00		
Plate, 8", rare	500.00			475.00		
Wine, very rare				400.00		
Panelled Flowers						
Rose Bowl, Footed	75.00		45.00			
Nut Cup, Footed	85.00		50.00			
Panelled Holly						
Pitcher	850.00		600.00			
Tumbler	125.00		90.00			
Butter	400.00		300.00			
Sugar	275.00		195.00			
Creamer	160.00		125.00			
Spooner	160.00		125.00			
Bowl, Master	195.00		135.00			
Bowl, Sauce	75.00		50.00			
Shakers, pair	260.00		170.00			

	Blue	Green	White	Vaseline/Canary	Cranberry	Other
Novelty Bowl	85.00		60.00			
Panelled Sprig						
Cruet			135.00			
Toothpick Holder			95.00			
Shakers, pair			110.00			
Peacock Tail						
Tumbler, rare	85.00	90.00	70.00			
Peacocks (On the Fence)						
Bowl	275.00		150.00			350.00 Cobalt
Pearl Flowers						
Nut Bowl, Footed	50.00	45.00	35.00			
Novelty Bowl, Footed	60.00	50.00	30.00			
Rose Bowl, Footed	70.00	75.00	45.00			
Pearls & Scales						
Compote	65.00	60.00	40.00	75.00		80.00 Emerald
Rose Bowl, rare				90.00		
Piasa Bird						
Bowl	55.00		40.00			
Vase	70.00		60.00			
Rose Bowl	85.00		70.00			
Spittoon Whimsey	90.00		80.00			
Picadilly						
Basket, small		85.00				
Pinecones & Leaves						
Bowl			70.00			
Pineapple & Fan						
Vase				400.00		
Plain Jane						
Nappy, Footed	50.00					
Plain Panels						
Vase	45.00	40.00	30.00			
Plume Panels Variant						
Vase, very rare		250.00				
Poinsettia						
Pitcher, either shape	350.00 – 500.00	375.00 – 550.00	250.00 – 400.00		750.00 – 1,300.00	
Tumbler	75.00		45.00		125.00	
Syrup, various	300.00 – 700.00	350.00 – 750.00	200.00 – 450.00		450.00 – 900.00	

	Blue	Green	White	Vaseline/Canary	Cranberry	Other
Sugar Shaker	300.00	300.00	190.00		450.00	
Fruit Bowl	125.00	110.00	85.00		165.00	
Poinsettia Lattice **(Lattice & Poinsettia)**						
Bowl, scarce	150.00		90.00	140.00		
Polka Dot*						
Pitcher, rare	250.00		150.00		850.00	
Tumbler	70.00		35.00		110.00*	
Syrup	250.00		125.00		725.00*	
Sugar Shaker	195.00		145.00		295.00	
Toothpick Holder	425.00		295.00		525.00	
Shakers, pair	95.00		60.00		295.00*	
Cruet	395.00*		250.00*		750.00*	
Bowl, large	75.00		55.00		125.00	
Popsicle Sticks						
Bowl, Footed	55.00	50.00	40.00			
Pressed Coinspot **(#617 or Concave Columns)**						
Compote	65.00	75.00	50.00	70.00		
Card Tray	75.00	95.00	60.00	100.00		
Primrose (Daffodils Variant)						
Pitcher			900.00			
Prince Albert & Victoria						
Open Sugar	65.00		60.00			
Creamer, Footed	65.00		60.00			
Princess Diana						
Crimped Plate	65.00			60.00		
Butter	100.00			95.00		
Open Sugar	70.00			65.00		
Creamer	55.00			50.00		
Pitcher	125.00			115.00		
Tumbler	40.00			35.00		
Water Tray	55.00			50.00		
Bisquit Set (Jar & Plate, Complete)	90.00			95.00		
Salad Bowl	55.00			50.00		
Novelty Bowl	50.00			45.00		
Compote, metal base	145.00*			135.00		
Compote, large	85.00			90.00		
Prince William						
Open Sugar	65.00			60.00		
Creamer	65.00			60.00		

	Blue	Green	White	Vaseline/ Canary	Cranberry	Other
Oval Plate	50.00			50.00		
Pitcher	100.00			100.00*		
Tumbler	40.00			37.00*		
Pulled Loop						
Vase, scarce, 2 sizes	40.00 – 80.00	55.00 – 90.00	30.00 – 60.00			
Pump & Trough*						
Complete, 2 pieces	130.00		80.00	115.00		
Queen's Crown						
Bowl, small	40.00			45.00		
Compote, low	60.00					
Queen's Petticoat						
Vase	85.00					
Question Mark						
Compote	65.00	85.00	50.00			
Card Tray	75.00					
Quilted Pillow Sham						
Oval Butter	100.00			90.00		
Creamer	70.00			65.00		
Open Sugar	70.00			60.00		
Rayed Heart						
Compote	65.00	60.00				
Reflecting Diamonds						
Bowl	55.00	60.00	40.00			
Reflections						
Bowl	50.00	50.00	35.00			
Regal (Northwood's)						
Pitcher	300.00	285.00	190.00			
Tumbler	85.00	70.00	40.00			
Butter	225.00	175.00	125.00			
Sugar	135.00	90.00	70.00			
Creamer	100.00	60.00	50.00			
Spooner	90.00	60.00	50.00			
Bowl, Master	125.00	150.00	110.00			
Bowl, Sauce	35.00	40.00	20.00			
Cruet	800.00	800.00	700.00			
Shakers, pair	400.00	400.00	300.00			
Celery Vase	150.00	175.00	90.00			
Reverse Drapery						
Bowl	45.00	45.00	30.00			

	Blue	Green	White	Vaseline/ Canary	Cranberry	Other
Plate	90.00	85.00	55.00			
Vase	40.00	40.00	35.00			

Reverse Swirl

	Blue	Green	White	Vaseline/ Canary	Cranberry	Other
Pitcher	250.00		175.00	220.00	795.00	
Tumbler	60.00		30.00	50.00	90.00	
Butter	195.00		135.00	165.00	250.00	
Sugar	170.00		110.00	150.00	220.00	
Creamer	120.00		90.00	110.00	185.00	
Spooner	120.00		85.00	95.00	145.00	
Bowl, Master	70.00		40.00	55.00	85.00	
Bowl, Sauce	25.00		20.00	25.00	40.00	
Cruet	265.00		110.00	170.00	465.00	
Toothpick Holder	155.00		95.00	125.00	265.00	
Sugar Shaker	170.00		115.00	140.00	270.00	
Syrup	175.00		100.00	140.00	425.00	
Mustard Pot	80.00		45.00	70.00	100.00	
Water Bottle	145.00		95.00	135.00	190.00	
Finger Bowl	70.00		45.00		100.00	
Shakers, pair	90.00		60.00	90.00	165.00	
Custard Cup	50.00		35.00		150.00	
Mini-Lamp	360.00		195.00		300.00	
Celery Vase	165.00		100.00	150.00	200.00	
Cruet Set and Holder, 4 pieces	295.00		200.00		365.00	
Oil Lamp					525.00	

Rib & Big Thumprints

	Blue	Green	White	Vaseline/ Canary	Cranberry	Other
Vase	45.00	40.00	30.00			

Ribbed Coinspot

	Blue	Green	White	Vaseline/ Canary	Cranberry	Other
Pitcher, rare					1,050.00	
Tumbler, rare					170.00	
Syrup, rare					1,375.00	
Celery Vase, rare					295.00	
Creamer, rare					495.00	
Sugar Shaker					550.00	

Ribbed Lattice

	Blue	Green	White	Vaseline/ Canary	Cranberry	Other
Pitcher	275.00		220.00		975.00	
Tumbler	50.00		40.00		150.00	
Cruet	225.00		165.00		495.00	
Shakers, pair	130.00		90.00		295.00	
Syrup	175.00		140.00		600.00	
Butter	215.00		175.00		800.00	
Sugar	120.00		95.00		650.00	
Creamer	75.00		65.00		400.00	
Spooner	75.00		65.00		400.00	
Bowl, Master	70.00		45.00		140.00	
Bowl, Sauce	30.00		20.00		35.00	

	Blue	Green	White	Vaseline/ Canary	Cranberry	Other
Toothpick Holder	295.00		160.00		300.00	
Sugar Shaker, 2 sizes	140.00		90.00		410.00	

Ribbed Opal Rings

	Blue	Green	White	Vaseline/ Canary	Cranberry	Other
Pitcher, rare					825.00	
Tumbler					115.00	

Ribbed Spiral

	Blue	Green	White	Vaseline/ Canary	Cranberry	Other
Pitcher	500.00		365.00	465.00		
Tumbler	115.00		60.00	100.00		
Butter	375.00		295.00	350.00		
Sugar	200.00		150.00	175.00		
Creamer	95.00		45.00	65.00		
Spooner	110.00		55.00	75.00		
Bowl, Master	75.00		45.00	65.00		
Bowl, Sauce	30.00		20.00	26.00		
Plate	75.00		45.00	60.00		
Cup/Saucer set	110.00		60.00	90.00		
Toothpick Holder	175.00		135.00	165.00		
Shakers, pair	210.00		135.00	200.00		
Jelly Compote	70.00		50.00	65.00		
Bowl	55.00		40.00	50.00		
Vase, many sizes	40.00 – 90.00		30.00 – 60.00	40.00 – 80.00		
Whimsey, 3-handled				120.00*		

Richelieu

	Blue	Green	White	Vaseline/ Canary	Cranberry	Other
Jelly Compote	75.00		55.00	70.00		
Bowl	70.00		50.00	65.00		
Creamer	65.00		45.00	60.00		
Open Sugar	65.00		45.00	60.00		
Divided Dish, rare	95.00		75.00	90.00		
Cracker Jar w/lid	195.00		165.00	185.00		
Basket, Handled	90.00		60.00	80.00		
Nappy, Handled	85.00		70.00	85.00		

Ring Handle

	Blue	Green	White	Vaseline/ Canary	Cranberry	Other
Shakers, pair	100.00		70.00			
Ring Tray	100.00	90.00	70.00			

Rippled Rib

	Blue	Green	White	Vaseline/ Canary	Cranberry	Other
Vase			40.00			

Rose Show

	Blue	Green	White	Vaseline/ Canary	Cranberry	Other
Bowl	275.00					

Rose Spray

	Blue	Green	White	Vaseline/ Canary	Cranberry	Other
Compote	50.00		35.00			60.00 Amethyst

Roulette

	Blue	Green	White	Vaseline/ Canary	Cranberry	Other
Novelty Bowl	50.00	45.00	35.00			

	Blue	Green	White	Vaseline/ Canary	Cranberry	Other
Ruffles & Rings						
Novelty Bowl	50.00	45.00	35.00			
Nut Bowl	55.00	50.00	40.00			
Rose Bowl	60.00	55.00	45.00			
Ruffles & Rings with Daisy Band						
Bowl, Footed			65.00			
S-Repeat						
Pitcher	500.00*		350.00*			
Tumbler	65.00		45.00			
Bowl, Master	85.00	95.00	70.00			
Scheherezade						
Novelty Bowl	50.00	47.00	35.00			
Scottish Moor						
Pitcher	350.00		275.00		475.00	400.00 Rubina
Tumbler	80.00		65.00		100.00	95.00 Amethyst
Cruet	395.00		225.00			
Cracker Jar	350.00		210.00			
Celery Vase	150.00		95.00			
Fluted Vase	140.00		95.00			
Scroll With Acanthus						
Pitcher	395.00	350.00		350.00		
Tumbler	90.00	75.00		75.00		
Butter	370.00	350.00		350.00		
Sugar	170.00	150.00		135.00		
Creamer	90.00	70.00		75.00		
Spooner	85.00	75.00		70.00		
Bowl, Master	55.00	55.00		50.00		
Bowl, Sauce	25.00	25.00		25.00		
Jelly Compote	65.00	60.00		60.00		
Toothpick Holder	285.00	275.00		310.00		
Cruet	225.00	220.00		375.00		
Shakers, pair	210.00	195.00		200.00		
Seafoam						
Compote	275.00		200.00			
Seaspray						
Nappy	47.00	45.00	37.00			
Seaweed						
Pitcher	350.00		250.00		425.00	
Tumbler	65.00		40.00		110.00	
Butter	200.00		120.00		395.00	
Sugar	165.00		135.00		210.00	
Creamer	125.00		95.00		200.00	

	Blue	Green	White	Vaseline/ Canary	Cranberry	Other
Spooner	125.00		90.00		175.00	
Bowl, Master	60.00		40.00		125.00	
Bowl, Sauce	30.00		20.00		70.00	
Cruet, 2 shapes	250.00		140.00		695.00	
Syrup	175.00		135.00		525.00	
Sugar Shaker	215.00		170.00		425.00	
Toothpick Holder	325.00		235.00		500.00	
Celery Vase	100.00		80.00		175.00	
Shakers, pair	150.00		110.00		350.00	
Barber Bottle, 2 shapes	180.00		110.00		300.00	
Mini-Lamp	500.00		375.00		1,850.00	
Pickle Castor, complete					500.00	
Rose Bowl			500.00*			

Shell, Beaded

	Blue	Green	White	Vaseline/ Canary	Cranberry	Other
Pitcher	560.00	625.00	495.00			
Tumbler	90.00	115.00	75.00			
Butter	500.00	675.00	425.00			
Sugar	225.00	260.00	185.00			
Creamer	150.00	180.00	145.00			
Spooner	150.00	180.00	145.00			
Bowl, Master	85.00	100.00	70.00			
Bowl, Sauce	55.00	65.00	40.00			
Cruet	500.00	695.00	400.00			
Toothpick Holder	475.00	675.00	500.00			
Shakers, pair	350.00	400.00	295.00			
Condiment set, 4 pc.	800.00	900.00	700.00			

Shell & Dots

	Blue	Green	White	Vaseline/ Canary	Cranberry	Other
Rose Bowl	47.00		35.00			
Novelty Bowl	52.00		40.00			

Shell & Wild Rose

	Blue	Green	White	Vaseline/ Canary	Cranberry	Other
Novelty Bowl, Open-edge	60.00	55.00	45.00			

Simple Simon

	Blue	Green	White	Vaseline/ Canary	Cranberry	Other
Compote	65.00	60.00	45.00			

Singing Birds

	Blue	Green	White	Vaseline/ Canary	Cranberry	Other
Mug, rare	350.00			600.00*		

Single Lily Spool

	Blue	Green	White	Vaseline/ Canary	Cranberry	Other
Epergne	95.00	90.00	70.00			

Sir Lancelot

	Blue	Green	White	Vaseline/ Canary	Cranberry	Other
Bowl, Footed	67.00	65.00	45.00			

Snowflake

	Blue	Green	White	Vaseline/ Canary	Cranberry	Other
Night Lamp	1,300.00*		795.00*		1,795.00	
Hand Lamp	395.00*		275.00*		600.00	

	Blue	Green	White	Vaseline/ Canary	Cranberry	Other
Oil Lamp	325.00*		220.00*		550.00	
Somerset						
Pitcher, Juice, 5½"	60.00		50.00			
Tumbler, 3"	30.00		26.00			
Oval Dish, 9"	45.00		37.00			
Square Dish	50.00		45.00			
Sowerby Salt						
Salt Dish	65.00	70.00	60.00			
Spanish Lace*						
Pitcher	250.00 – 500.00		110.00 – 300.00	220.00 – 450.00	650.00 – 1,000.00	
Tumbler	60.00		40.00	55.00	110.00	
Butter	410.00		220.00	395.00	500.00	
Sugar	260.00		195.00	250.00	320.00	
Spooner	140.00		90.00	130.00	175.00	
Creamer	140.00		90.00	125.00	175.00	
Bowl, Master	90.00		65.00	80.00	150.00	
Bowl, Sauce	30.00		25.00	30.00	40.00	
Syrup	250.00		175.00	350.00	650.00	
Sugar Shaker	150.00		100.00	140.00	200.00	
Celery Vase	120.00		85.00	135.00	175.00	
Shakers, pair	110.00		75.00	115.00	220.00	
Finger Bowl	70.00		55.00	85.00	150.00	
Bride's Basket, 2 sizes	125.00		90.00	140.00	200.00	
Jam Jar	290.00		195.00	325.00	500.00	
Cracker Jar	700.00				900.00	
Perfume Bottle	190.00		100.00	215.00	270.00	
Mini-Lamp	200.00		130.00	210.00	350.00	
Water Bottle	300.00		195.00	320.00	425.00	
Vase, many sizes	95.00		50.00	105.00	210.00	
Rose Bowl, many sizes	75.00		50.00	70.00	140.00	
Cruet	275.00		195.00	295.00	750.00	
Liquer Jug					850.00	
Spokes & Wheels						
Bowl	55.00	50.00	37.00			
Plate, rare	85.00	80.00				125.00 Aqua
Spool						
Compote	45.00	45.00	35.00			
Squirrel & Acorn						
Vase	90.00	80.00	75.00			
Bowl	85.00	75.00	70.00			
Compote	90.00	80.00	75.00			
Whimsey	90.00	85.00	75.00			

	Blue	Green	White	Vaseline/ Canary	Cranberry	Other
Stag & Holly						
Bowl, Footed, rare			200.00*			
Stars & Stripes*						
Pitcher			240.00		1,100.00	
Tumbler	100.00		70.00			
Lamp Shade			65.00			
Barber Bottle			100.00		295.00	
Compote, age uncertain					375.00	
Stork & Rushes						
Mug	95.00					
Tumbler			60.00			
Stork & Swan						
Syrup			150.00			
Strawberry						
Bon-Bon			220.00*			
Bowl						100.00 Amethyst
Stripe*						
Pitcher	275.00				560.00	
Tumbler	55.00				90.00	
Syrup	275.00				450.00	
Toothpick Holder	250.00				395.00	
Condiment Set	395.00				750.00*	
Barber Bottle	160.00				295.00	
Shakers, pair	100.00				250.00	
Rose Bowl	90.00				200.00	
Oil Lamp					600.00	
Bowl			60.00		100.00	
Vase			60.00		120.00	
Cruet					500.00 – 750.00	
Stripe, Wide						
Pitcher	250.00		160.00		450.00	
Tumbler	60.00		40.00		100.00	
Syrup	220.00		180.00		325.00	
Sugar Shaker	175.00		150.00		260.00	
Cruet	195.00	500.00	160.00		550.00	
Toothpick Holder	265.00	400.00	210.00		350.00	
Shakers, pair			140.00		240.00	
Sunburst On Shield (Diadem)						
Pitcher	600.00			950.00		
Tumbler	125.00			200.00		
Bowl, Master	140.00			195.00		
Bowl, Sauce	35.00			40.00		
Breakfast Set, 2 pieces	185.00			250.00		

	Blue	Green	White	Vaseline/ Canary	Cranberry	Other
Nappy, rare	220.00			340.00		
Cruet, rare	325.00		350.00	750.00		
Butter	375.00		250.00	395.00		
Sugar	225.00		175.00	250.00		
Creamer	140.00		95.00	135.00		
Spooner	140.00		95.00	135.00		

Sunk Hollyhock

	Blue	Green	White	Vaseline/ Canary	Cranberry	Other
Bowl, rare				95.00*		

Sunk Honeycomb

	Blue	Green	White	Vaseline/ Canary	Cranberry	Other
Bowl, very rare				200.00*		

Surf Spray

	Blue	Green	White	Vaseline/ Canary	Cranberry	Other
Pickle Dish	60.00	55.00	40.00			

Swag With Brackets

	Blue	Green	White	Vaseline/ Canary	Cranberry	Other
Pitcher	295.00	280.00	195.00	275.00		
Tumbler	85.00	75.00	45.00	75.00		
Butter	265.00	250.00	195.00	250.00		
Sugar	140.00	135.00	75.00	130.00		
Creamer	95.00	85.00	55.00	80.00		
Spooner	95.00	110.00	55.00	100.00		
Bowl, Master	75.00	65.00	45.00	65.00		
Bowl, Sauce	35.00	35.00	25.00	30.00		
Toothpick Holder	350.00	295.00	240.00	290.00		
Shakers, pair	195.00	175.00	130.00	180.00		
Cruet	500.00	320.00	170.00	240.00		
Jelly Compote	60.00	55.00	35.00	50.00		
Bowl	50.00	45.00	30.00	45.00		
Whimsey Sugar	160.00*			160.00*		

Swastika

	Blue	Green	White	Vaseline/ Canary	Cranberry	Other
Pitcher	900.00	900.00	675.00		1,100.00*	
Tumbler	100.00	125.00	80.00		150.00	
Syrup	950.00	950.00	850.00		1,300.00	

Swirl

	Blue	Green	White	Vaseline/ Canary	Cranberry	Other
Pitcher, various	125.00 – 200.00	110.00 – 190.00	60.00 – 110.00	295.00	250.00 – 650.00	
Tumbler	30.00	27.00	16.00	45.00	95.00	
Butter	125.00	120.00	70.00		155.00	
Sugar	90.00	95.00	50.00		160.00	
Creamer	70.00	80.00	40.00		95.00	
Spooner	70.00	80.00	40.00		125.00	
Bowl, Master	50.00	55.00	45.00		75.00	
Bowl, Sauce	20.00	25.00	16.00		36.00	
Syrup	115.00	110.00	75.00		155.00	
Sugar Shaker	135.00	100.00	70.00		165.00	
Cruet, 2 sizes	165.00	195.00	100.00		285.00	
Shakers, pair	170.00	150.00	100.00		240.00	

	Blue	Green	White	Vaseline/ Canary	Cranberry	Other
Fingerbowl	65.00	60.00	37.00		95.00	
Toothpick Holder	110.00	120.00	70.00		145.00	
Mustard Jar	95.00	100.00	58.00		145.00	
Rose Bowl	60.00	70.00	40.00		90.00	
Celery Vase	75.00	85.00	55.00		140.00	
Custard Cup	40.00	50.00	30.00		75.00	
Water, Bitters & Bar						
Bottles, each	90.00 – 250.00	90.00 – 195.00	65.00 – 100.00		350.00 – 450.00	
Lampshade	100.00	90.00	40.00		175.00	
Cheese Dish			240.00		395.00	
Fingerlamp			350.00		600.00	
Cruet Set, complete					475.00	
Strawholder, rare	800.00		575.00		1,150.00	
Vase	60.00	65.00	37.00		150.00	

Swirling Maze

	Blue	Green	White	Vaseline/ Canary	Cranberry	Other
Pitcher, any, (avg.)	475.00	450.00	300.00		795.00	
Tumbler	60.00	55.00	30.00		95.00	
Salad Bowl	95.00	90.00	60.00		145.00	

Target

	Blue	Green	White	Vaseline/ Canary	Cranberry	Other
Vase		110.00				

Thistle Patch

	Blue	Green	White	Vaseline/ Canary	Cranberry	Other
Novelty, Footed			40.00			

Thousand Eye

	Blue	Green	White	Vaseline/ Canary	Cranberry	Other
Pitcher			90.00			
Tumbler			25.00			
Butter			125.00			
Sugar			90.00			
Creamer			75.00			
Spooner			75.00			
Celery Vase			90.00			
Cruet			140.00			
Shakers, pair			70.00			
Toothpick Holder			120.00			
Bottles, various			25.00 – 50.00			
Bowl, various			25.00 – 45.00			

Thread & Rib

	Blue	Green	White	Vaseline/ Canary	Cranberry	Other
Epergne	800.00	900.00	600.00	800.00		

Three Fingers & Panel

	Blue	Green	White	Vaseline/ Canary	Cranberry	Other
Bowl, Master, rare	95.00		70.00	95.00		
Bowl, Sauce, rare	35.00		25.00	35.00		

Three Fruits

	Blue	Green	White	Vaseline/ Canary	Cranberry	Other
Bowl, scarce	200.00		125.00			

	Blue	Green	White	Vaseline/ Canary	Cranberry	Other
Three Fruits w/Meander						
Bowl, Footed	175.00		110.00			
Tiny Tears						
Vase	50.00	45.00	35.00			
Tokyo*						
Pitcher	350.00	300.00	160.00			
Tumbler	75.00	70.00	45.00			
Butter	185.00	175.00	85.00			
Sugar	140.00	130.00	60.00			
Creamer	90.00	80.00	40.00			
Spooner	90.00	85.00	45.00			
Vase	55.00	50.00	35.00			
Cruet	185.00	180.00	90.00			
Syrup	150.00	145.00	70.00			
Jelly Compote	55.00	55.00	30.00			
Plate	70.00	70.00	35.00			
Bowl, Master	45.00	40.00	25.00			
Bowl, Sauce	30.00	30.00	15.00			
Shakers, pair	90.00	85.00	45.00			
Toothpick Holder	250.00	200.00	125.00			
Trailing Vine						
Novelty Bowl	60.00		40.00	55.00		
Tree of Love						
Novelty Bowl			40.00			
Compote			50.00			
Plate, rare			135.00*			
Tree Stump						
Mug	90.00	100.00	60.00			
Tree Trunk						
Vase	40.00	45.00	30.00			
Trout						
Bowl			150.00*			
Twig						
Vase, small, 5½"	65.00	75.00	50.00	70.00		
Vase, Panelled, 7"	85.00	90.00	65.00	80.00		
Twist (miniatures)						
Butter	270.00		170.00	260.00		
Sugar	140.00		80.00	130.00		
Creamer	85.00		45.00	80.00		
Spooner	85.00		50.00	80.00		

	Blue	Green	White	Vaseline/ Canary	Cranberry	Other	
Twisted Ribs							
Vase	45.00	40.00	30.00				
Twister							
Bowl	50.00	45.00	35.00				
Plate	95.00						
Venetian (Spider Web)							
Vase	75.00						
Victorian							
Vase, applied flowers and vine	150.00	165.00	110.00	155.00		175.00	Amber
Vintage, Northwood/Dugan							
Bowl	45.00	50.00	30.00				
Rose Bowl	55.00	60.00	35.00				
Plate	70.00	75.00	50.00				
Vintage Leaf, Fenton							
Bowl, rare	150.00						
Vulcan Variant							
Creamer	60.00*		50.00*				
Sugar	75.00*		65.00*				
Spooner	60.00*		50.00*				
Butter	120.00*		110.00*				
Waffle							
Epergne						750.00	Olive
War Of The Roses							
Bowl	70.00			65.00			
Boat Shape	120.00						
Waterlily & Cattails							
Pitcher	420.00	395.00	250.00			425.00	Amethyst
Tumbler	70.00	60.00	30.00			80.00	Amethyst
Butter	395.00	350.00	240.00			410.00	Amethyst
Sugar	200.00	150.00	100.00			220.00	Amethyst
Creamer	100.00	75.00	60.00			110.00	Amethyst
Spooner	100.00	75.00	60.00			115.00	Amethyst
Bowl, Master	70.00	65.00	50.00			75.00	Amethyst
Bowl, Sauce	35.00	30.00	25.00			35.00	Amethyst
Novelty Bowl	45.00	40.00	30.00			55.00	Amethyst
Bon-Bon	70.00	65.00	45.00			80.00	Amethyst
Relish, Handled	95.00	90.00	70.00			120.00	Amethyst
Plate	90.00	85.00	60.00			100.00	Amethyst
Breakfast Set, 2 pcs.	145.00	135.00	100.00			165.00	Amethyst
Gravy Boat, Handled	60.00	55.00	40.00			75.00	Amethyst

	Blue	Green	White	Vaseline/ Canary	Cranberry	Other
Wheel & Block						
Novelty Bowl	45.00	40.00	30.00			
Vase Whimsey	55.00	45.00	35.00			
Novelty Plate	125.00	95.00	65.00			
Wide Panel						
Epergne, 4 Lily	800.00	850.00	600.00	900.00 rare		
Wild Bouquet						
Pitcher	275.00	240.00	190.00			
Tumbler	120.00	100.00	40.00			
Butter	495.00	450.00	325.00			
Sugar	295.00	260.00	185.00			
Creamer	195.00	150.00	100.00			
Spooner	195.00	150.00	100.00			
Bowl, Master	195.00	165.00	95.00			
Bowl, Sauce	60.00	50.00	40.00			
Cruet	395.00	425.00	250.00			
Toothpick Holder	425.00	375.00	225.00			
Shakers, pair	180.00	170.00	125.00			
Cruet Set w/tray	475.00	425.00	300.00			
Jelly Compote	160.00	130.00	90.00			
Wild Daffodils						
Mug	80.00		60.00			95.00 Amethyst 150.00 Custard Opal
Wild Rose						
Bowl	60.00		40.00			
Banana Bowl	70.00		50.00			
William & Mary						
Creamer	65.00			60.00		
Open Sugar, stemmed	70.00			65.00		
Master Salt	50.00					
Compote	95.00			90.00		
Cake Plate, stemmed	140.00			130.00		
Plate	100.00			95.00		
Wilted Flowers						
Bowl	50.00	60.00	40.00			
Windflower						
Bowl, rare	165.00		120.00			
Windows (Plain)*						
Pitcher, various	130.00 – 190.00		85.00 – 135.00		350.00 – 550.00	
Tumbler	55.00		35.00		110.00	
Mini Lamp	165.00				1,800.00	
Fingerbowl	50.00		47.00		75.00	
Oil Lamp					600.00	

	Blue	Green	White	Vaseline/ Canary	Cranberry	Other
Shade	60.00		35.00		195.00	
Barber Bottle					325.00	
Toothpick Holder					325.00	
Windows (Swirled)						
Pitcher, various	300.00 – 400.00		200.00 – 300.00		600.00 – 800.00	
Tumbler	85.00		65.00		120.00	
Butter	400.00		300.00		550.00	
Sugar	250.00		170.00		350.00	
Creamer	90.00		70.00		225.00	
Spooner	90.00		70.00		225.00	
Bowl, Master	55.00		40.00		95.00	
Bowl, Sauce	30.00		25.00		55.00	
Toothpick Holder	300.00		175.00		375.00	
Mustard Jar	75.00		55.00		150.00	
Cruet	310.00		220.00		475.00	
Sugar Shaker	150.00		110.00		325.00	
Syrup, 2 shapes	295.00		195.00		500.00	
Shakers, pair	165.00		120.00		295.00	
Cruet Set, complete	265.00		195.00		600.00	
Celery Vase	90.00		50.00		165.00	
Plate, 2 sizes	110.00		65.00		250.00	
Barber Bottle					325.00	
Winged Scroll						
Nappy, rare				150.00		
Winter Cabbage						
Bowl, Footed	47.00	45.00	36.00			
Winterlily						
Vase			50.00			
Wishbone & Drapery						
Bowl	47.00	42.00	36.00			
Plate	60.00	57.00	50.00			
Woven Wonder						
Rose Bowl	60.00		40.00			
Novelty Bowl	55.00		38.00			
Wreath & Shell						
Pitcher	595.00		195.00	365.00		
Tumbler, Flat or Footed	110.00		50.00	70.00		
Butter	250.00		135.00	210.00		
Sugar	200.00		95.00	150.00		
Creamer	160.00		80.00	130.00		
Spooner	160.00		80.00	120.00		
Bowl, Master	95.00		70.00	110.00		
Bowl, Sauce	37.00		25.00	32.00		

	Blue		Green	White	Vaseline/ Canary	Cranberry	Other
Celery Vase	180.00			100.00	160.00		
Rose Bowl	95.00			65.00	80.00		
Toothpick Holder	295.00			195.00	265.00		
Ladies Spittoon	95.00			65.00	115.00		
Cracker Jar	595.00			460.00	540.00		
Salt Dip	130.00			85.00	95.00		
Novelty Bowl	70.00			55.00	65.00		

Note: Add 10% for decorated items.

Wreathed Cherry*

	Blue		Green	White	Vaseline/ Canary	Cranberry	Other
Butter	85.00						
Creamer	70.00						
Sugar	75.00						
Spooner	60.00						

Note: Age questionable on all pieces.

Zipper & Loops

	Blue		Green	White	Vaseline/ Canary	Cranberry	Other
Vase, Footed	60.00		65.00	47.00			

Books on Antiques and Collectibles

This is only a partial listing of the books on antiques that are available from Collector Books. All books are well illustrated and contain current values. Most of the following books are available from your local book seller, antique dealer, or public library. If you are unable to locate certain titles in your area, you may order by mail from COLLECTOR BOOKS, P.O. Box 3009, Paducah, KY 42002-3009. Customers with Visa or MasterCard may phone in orders from 8:00–4:00 CST, Monday–Friday, Toll Free 1-800-626-5420. Add $2.00 for postage for the first book ordered and $0.30 for each additional book. Include item number, title, and price when ordering. Allow 14 to 21 days for delivery.

BOOKS ON GLASS AND POTTERY

1810	American Art Glass, Shuman	$29.95
1312	Blue & White Stoneware, McNerney	$9.95
1959	Blue Willow, 2nd Ed., Gaston	$14.95
3719	Coll. Glassware from the 40's, 50's, 60's, 2nd Ed., Florence	$19.95
3816	Collectible Vernon Kilns, Nelson	$24.95
3311	Collecting Yellow Ware – Id. & Value Gd., McAllister	$16.95
1373	Collector's Ency. of American Dinnerware, Cunningham	$24.95
3815	Coll. Ency. of Blue Ridge Dinnerware, Newbound	$19.95
2272	Collector's Ency. of California Pottery, Chipman	$24.95
3811	Collector's Ency. of Colorado Pottery, Carlton	$24.95
1312	Collector's Ency. of Children's Dishes, Whitmyer	$19.95
2133	Collector's Ency. of Cookie Jars, Roerig	$24.95
3723	Coll. Ency. of Cookie Jars-Volume II, Roerig	$24.95
3724	Collector's Ency. of Depression Glass, 11th Ed., Florence	$19.95
2209	Collector's Ency. of Fiesta, 7th Ed., Huxford	$19.95
1439	Collector's Ency. of Flow Blue China, Gaston	$19.95
3812	Coll. Ency. of Flow Blue China, 2nd Ed., Gaston	$24.95
3813	Collector's Ency. of Hall China, 2nd Ed., Whitmyer	$24.95
2334	Collector's Ency. of Majolica Pottery, Katz-Marks	$19.95
1358	Collector's Ency. of McCoy Pottery, Huxford	$19.95
3313	Collector's Ency. of Niloak, Gifford	$19.95
1837	Collector's Ency. of Nippon Porcelain I, Van Patten	$24.95
2089	Collector's Ency. of Nippon Porcelain II, Van Patten	$24.95
1665	Collector's Ency. of Nippon Porcelain III, Van Patten	$24.95
1447	Collector's Ency. of Noritake, 1st Series, Van Patten	$19.95
1034	Collector's Ency. of Roseville Pottery, Huxford	$19.95
1035	Collector's Ency. of Roseville Pottery, 2nd Ed., Huxford	$19.95
3314	Collector's Ency. of Van Briggle Art Pottery, Sasicki	$24.95
1433	Collector's Guide To Harker Pottery - U.S.A., Colbert	$17.95
2339	Collector's Guide to Shawnee Pottery, Vanderbilt	$19.95
1425	Cookie Jars, Westfall	$9.95
3440	Cookie Jars, Book II, Westfall	$19.95
2275	Czechoslovakian Glass & Collectibles, Barta	$16.95
3882	Elegant Glassware of the Depression Era, 6th Ed., Florence	$19.95
3725	Fostoria - Pressed, Blown & Hand Molded Shapes, Kerr	$24.95
3883	Fostoria Stemware - The Crystal for America, Long	$24.95
3886	Kitchen Glassware of the Depression Years, 5th Ed., Florence	$19.95
3889	Pocket Guide to Depression Glass, 9th Ed., Florence	$9.95
1825	Puritan Pottery, Morris	$24.95
1670	Red Wing Collectibles, DePasquale	$9.95
1440	Red Wing Stoneware, DePasquale	$9.95
1958	So. Potteries Blue Ridge Dinnerware, 3rd Ed., Newbound	$14.95
3739	Standard Carnival Glass, 4th Ed., Edwards	$24.95
3327	Watt Pottery – Identification & Value Guide, Morris	$19.95
2224	World of Salt Shakers, 2nd Ed., Lechner	$24.95

BOOKS ON DOLLS & TOYS

2079	Barbie Fashion, Vol. 1, 1959-1967, Eames	$24.95
3310	Black Dolls - 1820 - 1991 – Id. & Value Guide, Perkins	$17.95
1810	Chatty Cathy Dolls, Lewis	$15.95
1529	Collector's Ency. of Barbie Dolls, DeWein	$19.95
2338	Collector's Ency. of Disneyana, Longest & Stern	$24.95
3727	Coll. Guide to Ideal Dolls, Izen	$18.95
1822	Madame Alexander Price Guide #19, Smith	$9.95
3732	Matchbox Toys, 1948 to 1993, Johnson	$18.95

3733	Modern Collector's Dolls, 6th series, Smith	$24.95
1540	Modern Toys, 1930 - 1980, Baker	$19.95
3824	Patricia Smith's Doll Values – Antique to Modern, 10th ed	$12.95
3826	Story of Barbie, Westenhouser, No Values	$19.95
2028	Toys, Antique & Collectible, Longest	$14.95
1808	Wonder of Barbie, Manos	$9.95
1430	World of Barbie Dolls, Manos	$9.95

OTHER COLLECTIBLES

1457	American Oak Furniture, McNerney	$9.95
3716	American Oak Furniture, Book II, McNerney	$12.95
2333	Antique & Collectible Marbles, 3rd Ed., Grist	$9.95
1748	Antique Purses, Holiner	$19.95
1426	Arrowheads & Projectile Points, Hothem	$7.95
1278	Art Nouveau & Art Deco Jewelry, Baker	$9.95
1714	Black Collectibles, Gibbs	$19.95
1128	Bottle Pricing Guide, 3rd Ed., Cleveland	$7.95
3717	Christmas Collectibles, 2nd Ed., Whitmyer	$24.95
1752	Christmas Ornaments, Johnston	$19.95
3718	Collectible Aluminum, Grist	$16.95
2132	Collector's Ency. of American Furniture, Vol. I, Swedberg	$24.95
2271	Collector's Ency. of American Furniture, Vol. II, Swedberg	$24.95
3720	Coll. Ency. of American Furniture, Vol III, Swedberg	$24.95
3722	Coll. Ency. of Compacts, Carryalls & Face Powder Boxes, Mueller	$24.95
2018	Collector's Ency. of Granite Ware, Greguire	$24.95
3430	Coll. Ency. of Granite Ware, Book 2, Greguire	$24.95
1441	Collector's Guide to Post Cards, Wood	$9.95
2276	Decoys, Kangas	$24.95
1629	Doorstops – Id. & Values, Bertoia	$9.95
1716	Fifty Years of Fashion Jewelry, Baker	$19.95
3817	Flea Market Trader, 9th Ed., Huxford	$12.95
3731	Florence's Standard Baseball Card Price Gd., 6th Ed.	$9.95
3819	General Store Collectibles, Wilson	$24.95
3436	Grist's Big Book of Marbles, Everett Grist	$19.95
2278	Grist's Machine Made & Contemporary Marbles	$9.95
1424	Hatpins & Hatpin Holders, Baker	$9.95
3884	Huxford's Collectible Advertising – Id. & Value Gd., 2nd Ed	$24.95
3820	Huxford's Old Book Value Guide, 6th Ed.	$19.95
3821	Huxford's Paperback Value Guide	$19.95
1181	100 Years of Collectible Jewelry, Baker	$9.95
2216	Kitchen Antiques – 1790 - 1940, McNerney	$14.95
3887	Modern Guns – Id. & Val. Gd., 10th Ed., Quertermous	$12.95
3734	Pocket Guide to Handguns, Quertermous	$9.95
3735	Pocket Guide to Rifles, Quertermous	$9.95
3736	Pocket Guide to Shotguns, Quertermous	$9.95
2026	Railroad Collectibles, 4th Ed., Baker	$14.95
1632	Salt & Pepper Shakers, Guarnaccia	$9.95
1888	Salt & Pepper Shakers II, Guarnaccia	$14.95
2220	Salt & Pepper Shakers III, Guarnaccia	$14.95
3443	Salt & Pepper Shakers IV, Guarnaccia	$18.95
3890	Schroeder's Antiques Price Guide, 13th Ed.	$12.95
2096	Silverplated Flatware, 4th Ed., Hagan	$14.95
2348	20th Century Fashionable Plastic Jewelry, Baker	$19.95
3828	Value Guide to Advertising Memorabilia, Summers	$18.95
3830	Vintage Vanity Bags & Purses, Gerson	$24.95

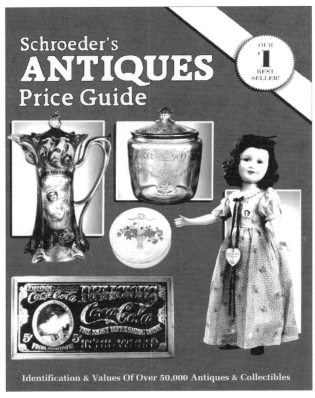